To Carrol Dexter and
Charlotte Devereaux,
with love

WHY NOT CATCH-21?

The Stories Behind the Titles

GARY DEXTER

FRANCES LINCOLN LIMITED
PUBLISHERS

WHY NOT CATCH-21?

Frances Lincoln Limited
4 Torriano Mews
Torriano Avenue
London NW5 2RZ
www.franceslincoln.com

First Frances Lincoln edition: 2007
First paperback edition: 2008

Hardback ISBN: 978-0-7112-2796-5
Paperback ISBN: 978-0-7112-2925-9

Printed in the UK by CPI Bookmarque, Croydon, CR0 4TD

2 4 6 8 9 7 5 3 1

CONTENTS

FOREWORD

Most book titles simply describe the contents of the book they are attached to. *Crime and Punishment* is about crime and punishment, and *Brideshead Revisited* is about revisiting Brideshead. But a small number of book titles have a rather odd, separate existence, almost as independent literary artefacts. The stories behind them are quite different from the stories behind the actual books. *Winnie-the-Pooh*, for example, is to do with a swan on a pond at a holiday cottage. *The Postman Always Rings Twice* is about the travails of a screenwriter. And *Catch-22* only got that way after a clash with another author, and via a route that included several other numbers.

Even in cases where titles are purely descriptive there can be more to say. *The Picture of Dorian Gray* seems pretty straightforward until you realize that there was a real young man called Dorian Gray, whose life story was rather different from his 'picture'. There was also a real Doctor Faustus, a real Duchess of Malfi, a real Hamlet, a real Moby-Dick and a real Oleanna (though she was a place, not a person).

This book grew out of a weekly column for *The Sunday Telegraph* called 'Title Deed'. In it I set myself four conditions for inclusion, as I do in this book. First, each title should be the title of a book, rather than, say, a poem. Secondly, the title should not be explicable by reading the text of the book itself. Thirdly, no quotations as sources for titles. Fourthly, the explanation for the title should not be very well known.

I have relied on the efforts of a great many scholars to write this book, and a list of sources is given at the end. I also owe a great debt to Miriam Gross, who originally commissioned *The Sunday Telegraph* column, and to Michael Prodger, who kept it going.

I. THE REPUBLIC
(*c.*380 BC)

If Plato could be put into a time machine and brought to the twenty-first century, he would find many things to surprise him. Electricity, votes for women, competitive hot-dog eating – and the title of his most famous work, *The Republic*. For a start, he would not understand it: it's Latin, not Greek. And if someone translated it for him, he would probably be rather astonished to find it attached to his book.

It is difficult to say what a republic is. Such differing modern states as China, the Congo, Brazil and the USA are all republics. If they share anything, it is probably only the aspiration that government should be free of unelected individuals or bodies. There are no republican monarchies: republicanism is, in theory, democratic, deriving power from electors.

So when we open Plato's *Republic*, we expect that the topic under discussion will be how to run a Greek city-state so as best to reflect the wishes of the people. A primer, in short, of that invention of the Greeks, democracy.

But Plato loathed democracy. Democracy, for him, was one step above tyranny. Democrats had killed the man he admired most in the world, Socrates. *The Republic* is an argument not for, but against democracy.

Plato was writing in about 380 BC, in the wake of a series of political disasters in Athens. The era of the Athenian Empire under Pericles had recently passed away and there had been a disastrous war against Syracuse in 412. An oligarchy had taken over and this, in turn, had been displaced by the democratic faction, which had ordered a series of bloody reprisals. These struggles were all witnessed by the young Plato, who would then have been in his twenties. Towards the end of his life he wrote of the fate of Socrates under the democrats: 'Unfortunately, however, some of those in power brought my friend Socrates to trial on a monstrous charge, the last that could be made against him, the charge of impiety; and he was condemned and executed.'

The Republic was an early attempt by Plato to pick over the tragedy of Socrates and understand it. It was told in the first person, not in Plato's own voice, but in that of Socrates. The book was titled in Greek *Politeia*, which referred to the *polis*, or city-state, and can be rendered 'the state', 'affairs of the state' or, more broadly, 'the life of the people'. Foreign translations give some idea of how far the title of *The Republic* has strayed from its origins: it is *Der Stadt* in German, *De Staat* in Dutch, *Stat* in Slovak, *Ustava* ('Constitution') in Czech and *Valsts* ('the State') in Latvian. The book was intended as a manual on the good governance of a particular type of Greek political unit. It explored the political models on offer at the time, rejected all of them, and came to one, single, surprising conclusion.

Of the available models, timarchy was judged to be the best of a bad bunch. This was the system currently prevailing in Sparta, in which a small class of landed warriors lived amidst a slave population, the helots, subduing them by means of military dictatorship and athletics. Oligarchy, the next most desirable, was government by a wealthy minority of unelected bureaucrat-politicians. The next was democracy, in which there was government by popular demagogues.[1] The lowest of all, tyranny, was a state in which one terribly unhappy man, 'surrounded by boyfriends and girlfriends', enacted the destruction of the state through his own personal moral degradation.

Socrates/Plato, having demolished the opposition, then described his ideal state. This was an entirely theoretical polity, one ruled by 'Guardians', or specially trained philosopher-rulers. The Guardians, unelected and set apart from the rest of the population (the Workers) from birth, would be bred eugenically by means of 'marriage festivals' (in fact state-sponsored orgies, since marriage was not their main purpose, but acts of intercourse by the fittest individuals). They would receive philosophical training for fifty years before being allowed to emerge and govern. They were expected 'to come to their duties with the least enthusiasm', since 'the state whose rulers are eager to rule are the worst.' A sub-set of the Guardians were the Auxiliaries, who would exist to keep order and prosecute wars. In order to keep the Workers loyal, a founding myth (sometimes translated as a 'noble lie') would be deliberately fabricated, the 'myth of Er'.

Some commentators have seen the whole of *The Republic* as a huge joke, and certainly in the book Socrates' ideas are met with incredulity. Glaucon (in real life Plato's older brother) says: 'My dear Socrates, if you produce theories of that sort, you can't be surprised if most decent people take their coats off, pick up the nearest weapon, and come after you in their shirt sleeves to do something terrible to you.' It was precisely what had recently happened to Socrates.

The title of *The Republic*, then, is rather strange: Plato's ideal state is about as far away from representative republican democracy as it is possible to get. The reason lies essentially in the very great swathes of time that have elapsed since it was first translated. In its first Latin translation the title was *Respublica*, a word similar in meaning to Plato's *Politeia*, and signifying 'public matters' or 'matters of state'. (*De re publica*, a book in the Socratic dialogue style by the jurist and politician Cicero, also dealt with the proper organization of the *respublica*, that is the 'constitution' or 'society'.) Our modern word 'republic', meaning democratic government shorn of unelected bodies, evolved from the term *respublica*, and its evolution in meaning twisted the meaning of Plato's title. *The Republic* used to be a good translation, but evolved into a mistranslation.

For many centuries after Plato's death, up to the Enlightenment and beyond, *The Republic* was the key text of political philosophy. In the twentieth century however things began to change. Modern liberal humanitarians came to *The Republic* and found it crowded with strange totalitarian fantasies. Their reaction was one of revulsion. In Karl Popper's book *The Open Society and its Enemies*, Plato's government of philosopher-rulers is seen as insanely rigid and stratified, a migration of geometry into political theory. Two works of twentieth-century dystopianism also drew on *The Republic*: Huxley's *Brave New World* and Orwell's *Nineteen Eighty-Four*. In Huxley's book, the philosopher-rulers are represented by the World Controllers, with the 'marriage festivals' becoming eugenic breeding programmes; in *Nineteen Eighty-Four* there is an echo of Plato's Guardians and Auxiliaries in the Inner and Outer Party, with the third force, the Workers, becoming Orwell's Proles, and the myth of Er the slogans of Big Brother.

Alfred North Whitehead said that the whole of Western philosophy was 'a series of footnotes to Plato'. The rise of totalitarianism in the twentieth century seemed to be telling us that there was something rotten in the text at the heart of Western culture. Plato's book was a totalitarian text masquerading under a libertarian title. A better metaphor for the political misery we had created for ourselves could not be imagined.

1 Athenian democracy was not of course identical to modern democracy, but there were recognizable similarities, and perhaps more similarities than differences: it had an Assembly of adult male voters that met regularly, a Council of Five Hundred that represented them, and smaller Committees that thrashed out details of legislation and other business. Plato thought that democracy a) brought to the fore popular rulers who were chiefly concerned to maintain themselves in power and would do and say anything that helped achieve this end; b) did not take into consideration the ignorance and fickleness of voters on most matters of importance; and c) fostered dislike of authority and valued freedom over order.

2. UTOPIA
(1516)

When *Utopia* first appeared in print, some readers thought it was all true, and that Thomas More had simply copied down the reports of a traveller.[1]

After all, why not? There was nothing intrinsically impossible about *Utopia*. There were none of the monsters found in Pliny's *Natural History*, where some of the humans encountered have only one leg, and use their single foot as a sunshade. The book is presented as factual. It starts off by making references to real things, such as the goings-on at the courts of England and Holland, or the recent voyages of Amerigo Vespucci. When it continues with a description of a voyage to Utopia, and of the strange society found there, an inattentive reader could be forgiven for thinking that this new land was real, merely one among the many lands and continents being discovered in the early sixteenth century. Many of the features of Utopian society seem quite admirable. No one goes hungry in Utopia. There is free healthcare. Rulers are given the power to rule only if they show no appetite for it.[2] In the relations between the sexes, adultery is severely punished, but there is divorce by mutual consent, and prospective marriage partners are allowed to 'inspect the goods' before the wedding:

> In choosing their wives they use a method that would appear to us very absurd and ridiculous, but it is constantly observed among them, and is accounted perfectly consistent with wisdom. Before marriage some grave matron presents the bride, naked, whether she is a virgin or a widow, to the bridegroom, and after that some grave man presents the bridegroom, naked, to the bride.[3]

But reading rather more closely, and with a more ironic cast of mind, there were numerous clues to the book's nature as a literary rather than a journalistic production. One of the most obvious was in the title. In full it was *De Optimo Reipublicae Statu deque Nova Insula Utopia* ('On the Best Form of a Republic and on the New Island of Utopia'). The name 'Utopia' was More's neologism, and contained a double pun. It derived both from the Greek *ou topos*, 'no place', and *eu topos*, 'good place'. The double pun was explicitly invoked by More in an introductory poem, 'Lines on the Island of Utopia by the Poet Laureate Anemolius, Hythlodaeus's Sister's Son':

> UTOPIA was once my name,
> That is, a place where no one goes.
> Plato's Republic now I claim
> To match, or beat at its own game;
> For that was just a myth in prose,
> But what he wrote of, I became,
> Of men, wealth, laws a solid frame,
> A place where every wise man goes:
> EUTOPIA is now my name.[4]

The two terms 'Utopia' and 'Eutopia' suggest that the country is both good and nonexistent – too good to be true, one might say. Other names in the book also undermine the idea that what is being said is actually true or indeed sane: the traveller from whom More hears the report is Raphael Hythlodaeus, literally 'Raphael the dispenser of nonsense'. *Utopia* was written in Latin, and there are other Latin and Greek names that can be Englished as 'Tallstoria', 'Blindland' 'Nolandia', Aircastle', 'Nopeople' and 'Nowater'.[5]

So Sir Thomas in his *Utopia* was presenting a hopelessly mixed picture. Was he an early Communist who believed that property should be held in common and that money was the

curse of mankind? Passages such as this one towards the end of
the book lead us to think that, in moments, he might have been:

> In fact, when I consider any social system that prevails in
> the modern world, I can't, so help me God, see it as any-
> thing but a conspiracy of the rich to advance their own
> interests under the pretext of organizing society. They
> think up all sorts of tricks and dodges, first for keeping
> safe their ill-gotten gains, and then for exploiting the poor
> by buying their labour as cheaply as possible [. . .] Every-
> one could so easily get enough to eat, if it weren't for that
> blessed nuisance, money.

But then we encounter some piece of hyperbole such as that
Utopian chamber-pots are made out of precious metals (to
encourage contempt for wealth), or that Utopian women can
be ordained as priests (which More, as a sixteenth-century
Catholic, cannot have believed would be a good idea). Serious
political and social comment, often expressed with genuine
indignation, is side by side with satire and absurdity. It is rather
like reading *Private Eye*. Moralizing and parody rub shoulders.
It is an entertaining, invigorating and sometimes rather annoy-
ing conjunction.

But perhaps this mixed picture is the essence of *Utopia*, not
an isolated fault in it. The 'frame story' involving Raphael
Hythlodaeus gave More a golden licence to have fun with no
consequences. He could easily disclaim any or all of *Utopia*,
since it was not, after all, 'by him', but the report of a traveller.
It was rather like Plato using Socrates in *The Republic* to voice
opinions that were unpopular or dangerous or absurd. Utopia
was both a good place or a nonsensical place, either separately
or, if it took More's fancy, both at once. The book was a *jeu
d'esprit*, and the reader was expected to play along. Erasmus,
More's friend and admirer, very probably revealed the key to

Utopia when he said that More, famous for his sagacity throughout Europe, had also 'from earliest childhood such a passion for jokes, that one might almost suppose he had been born for them.'

1 More actively encouraged this supposition: *Utopia* has a 'frame story' in which More meets a traveller, who recounts the story of his sojourn in Utopia.
2 An idea found in Plato's *Republic*: see chapter 1. There are many references to Plato in *Utopia*.
3 This has an odd echo in a story about More in John Aubrey's *Brief Lives* of 1697. 'Sir William Roper, of Eltham, in Kent, came one morning, pretty early, to my Lord [i.e. More], with a proposal to marry one of his daughters. My Lord's daughters were then both together abed in a truckle bed in their father's chamber asleep. He carries Sir William into the chamber and takes the sheet by the corner and suddenly whips it off. They lay on their backs, and their smocks up as high as their armpits. This awakened them, and immediately they turned on their bellies. Quoth Roper, I have seen both sides, and so gave a pat on the buttock he made choice of, saying, Thou art mine. Here was all the trouble of the wooing. This account I had from my honoured friend old Mrs Tyndale, whose grandfather, Sir William Stafford, was an intimate friend of this Sir W. Roper, who told him the story.' This story was third-hand (or fourth, or fifth: Roper told Stafford, Stafford was Mrs Tyndale's *grandfather*, so it would have been a family story long before she heard it) and contains some unlikely details (would both of their smocks have been conveniently up at their armpits?).
4 The original text reads: 'UTOPIA priscis dicta ob infrequentiam/Nunc ciuitatis æmula Platonicæ . . . EUTOPIA merito sum vocanda nomine.' I have followed the translation by Paul Turner, but have altered his English versions of the place names 'Utopia' and 'Eutopia' – these being 'Noplacia' and 'Goplacia' – to give the original Latin names, for clarity.
5 As translated by Paul Turner.

3. GARGANTUA AND PANTAGRUEL
(1532)

Gargantua and Pantagruel, two giants, father and son, were created by the French doctor and monk François Rabelais in the mid-sixteenth century. The five books of their adventures stand at the beginning of a tradition of erudite nonsense later ornamented by Sterne, Swift, Carroll and Joyce. Gargantua's codpiece takes twenty-four yards of wool to make; when he pisses it drowns 260,418 Parisians (not including women and children); 11,900 pounds of rhubarb are required to ease his constipation; 17,913 cows must supply milk to wean him. Pantagruel can cover an army by letting out his tongue; with one fart he engenders 53,000 dwarves, which are sent to live on an island where they fight flocks of cranes; there are several cities in his mouth. And yet these prodigious monsters are at other times small and human enough to study at university, enter ordinary rooms by ordinary doors, ride a horse or sit in a chair. They are literary, rather than fairy-tale giants. Children, after all, generally ask for some sort of sense.

Rabelais is careful to give exact etymologies for their respective names. The origin of Gargantua is as follows:

> While that good man Grandgousier [Gargantua's father] was drinking and joking with the others he heard the horrible cry made by his son as he entered the world, bawling out for 'Drink! Drink! Drink!' Whereupon he said, '*Que grand tu as.*' – What a big one you've got! – (the gullet being understood); and when they heard this the company said that the child ought properly to be called Gargantua – after the example of the ancient

Hebrew custom – since that had been the first word pronounced by his father at his birth.

Pantagruel is explained thus:

And because Pantagruel was born on that very day, his father gave him the name he did: for *Panta* in Greek is equivalent to *all*, and *Gruel*, in the Hagarene language, is as much as to say *thirsty*; by this meaning to infer that at the hour of the child's nativity the world was all thirsty, and also seeing, in a spirit of prophecy, that one day his son would be ruler over the thirsty. . .

Both of these thirst-orientated explanations are side-swipes at the truth. The name Gargantua existed before Rabelais, in a popular book about a giant of that name published anonymously in the early 1500s, the *Great Chronicles of Gargantua*. The 'garg' of Gargantua does indeed have to do with the gullet, or throat: in the Provençal dialect, throat is *gargamallo* and in Languedocien it is *gargamela*. Gargantua's mother is called Gargamelle,[1] and his father, Grandgousier, takes his name from *gosier*, the French for 'throat'. Gargantua's family therefore derive their appellations, both in Rabelais's comic philology and in actuality, from the throat and from thirst. Pantagruel is the same. His name, Rabelais assures us, means 'all-thirsty'. But the ludicrous appeal to an origin in the 'Hagarene' language covers up the fact that his real source, again, is in popular literature and folklore. In Rabelais' time Penthagruel was a dwarf-devil who preyed on drunkards, throwing salt in their mouths while they were asleep so that they woke thirsty, hungover and dying for a glass of wine. Pantagruel is born during a drought and is preceded from the womb by a wagon train of thirst-inducing victuals. His mother, the poor giantess Badebec, is 'suffocated' by the effort of giving birth and expires.

So the unavoidable theme of the giants' names is drink, drinking, thirst, thirstiness, and the quenching of it with floods of life-giving wine. The preoccupation runs throughout the books. The tone is struck very early on. Rabelais begins Book I with an 'Author's Prologue' addressed to his readers, imagined as a bunch of drunks:

> Most noble boozers, and you my very esteemed and poxy friends [. . .] If you do not believe those arguments, what reason is there that you should not treat these new and jolly chronicles of mine with the same reserve, seeing that as I dictated them I gave no more thought to the matter than you, who were probably drinking at the time, as I was? [. . .] To be called a good companion and fellow-boozer is to me pure honour and glory.

Wine bubbles everywhere throughout Rabelais's work, an invigorating prelude, accompaniment and postscript to any and every activity. So much is consumed that when the giants relieve themselves, the streams of urine work waterwheels and wash away villages. In the Prologue to Book III, Rabelais's books are themselves conceived of as drink:

> Every honest boozer, every decent gouty gentleman, everyone who is dry, may come to this barrel of mine, but need drink only if he wishes. [. . .] Such is my statute; and have no fear that the wine will give out, as it did at the marriage at Cana in Galilee. As much as you draw out at the tap, I will pour in at the bung. In this way the cask will remain inexhaustible, endowed with a living spring and a perpetual flow.

Wine is literature, symbolic of the intoxication of learning; wine is companionship, necessary for the intercourse of man and man; wine is heretical salvation. The obsession with drinking culminates in a voyage to the Oracle of the Holy Bottle, the last chapter of the five books, where Panurge (Pantagruel's sidekick) wishes to get an answer to the question of whether or not he should get married. The Oracle's answer is one word – 'Trink!' The solution even to the basic problem of man and woman is liquid in nature.

Perhaps in the light of this we should redefine 'Rabelaisian'. Most of us think of it as denoting bawdiness or coarseness. The bawdy and scatological – two styles which are barely distinguishable from one another in Rabelais, the act of love being comically treated as a lusty evacuation – are present in great quantity throughout the 800 pages of *Gargantua and Pantagruel*. But they come a poor second and third to Rabelais's main preoccupation. Delight in bibulosity is the chief Rabelaisian characteristic, and it's right there in the title.

1 Gargamelle was also the name of a giant particle detector at CERN in Switzerland, built in the late 1960s and used for the detection of neutrinos.

4. ASTROPHIL AND STELLA
(*c.*1581)

On the morning of September 22, 1586, following an assault on Spanish forces outside the Dutch town of Zutphen, Sir Phillip Sidney was badly wounded in the thigh.[1] His friend and biographer Fulke Greville described how, returning with the English wounded,

> he called for drink, which was presently brought him; but as he was putting the bottle to his mouth, he saw a poor Souldier carryed along, who had eaten his last at the same Feast, gastly casting up his eyes at the bottle. Which Sir *Philip* perceiving, took it from his head, before he drank, and delivered it to the poor man, with these words, *Thy necessity is greater than mine.* And when he had pledged this poor souldier, he was presently carried to Arnheim.

He died in agony nearly a month later, of complications to the wound.

Philip Sidney was the epitome of a Protestant English knight: well born, young, valorous, a champion at the tilt, a rhetorician, a scholar and a favourite of the monarch. There was national grief at his death. 'And the whole nation went into mourning, and for many months it was counted a sin for any gentleman of quality to appear at Court, or in the City, in any light or gaudy apparel.'[2] Despite this Sir Philip would probably be forgotten today had it not been for his contribution to English literature. His *Defence of Poesie* was the first major sustained work of literary theory in English, and his prose work *Arcadia* presented a new and influential form of pastoral romance (Charles I is said to have quoted from it as he mounted the scaffold). His crowning literary achievement was *Astrophil and Stella*, which pioneered the English sonnet sequence. Sonnet-making had become popular in the early 1500s with the work of writers such as Thomas Wyatt and the Earl of Surrey, but *Astrophil and Stella* was the first attempt to create a sonnet sequence in English after the manner of Petrarch or Dante, a unified collection with a semi-dramatic progression of thought. It was the precursor of the sonnet sequences of Spenser and Shakespeare.

Astrophil and Stella was also a coded text reflecting an illicit love affair. Stella ('star') was Lady Penelope Devereaux, the fourteen-year-old to whom Philip had been promised in marriage. Astrophil, or 'star-lover', was Philip himself. The stellar theme was perfect for Philip, whose last name contained the first three letters of *sidus* (star) and whose first name was also present in truncated form as the 'phil' of Astrophil, a name that thus neatly united lover and beloved. That Philip intended a pun can be seen in another invented name, this time from the *Arcadia*, that of Philisides, 'lover of a star', a character also thought to represent Philip.

Lady Penelope was the daughter of Walter Devereaux, the first Earl of Essex. It was Walter's wish that Penelope be betrothed to Philip,[3] but Walter's death in 1576 sparked a series of events that was to lead to the reversal of Philip's hopes. In 1580, Walter's widow, Lettice Knollys, remarried, again into one of the great noble houses of England, becoming the wife of Robert Dudley, the first Earl of Leicester. Robert happened to be Philip's uncle, and Philip was his heir. Robert's marriage to Lettice thus effectively disinherited Philip, since within a very short time (in 1581) Robert and Lettice had produced their own male heir. They had also changed their mind about the betrothal of Penelope and Philip. In 1581 Penelope was married off to a better prospect,

Robert Rich, the Earl of Warwick. 1581 was therefore a cata-
strophic year for Philip. He had been both disinherited and
jilted. In that year he appeared at tilt with the word 'Speravi' –
'I hoped', written on his shield, but crossed out with a thick
line.

Astrophil and Stella is presented as a drama, in which 108
sonnets are interspersed with 11 songs. Astrophil loves Stella,
although she does not explicitly return his love. The poet
begins by appealing to the moon, praising his loved one's
beauty, bemoaning his fate and her indifference, toying with
ideas to do with the nature of true virtue, true love and true
wisdom. Then the wedding to Rich is announced and in
sonnet 37 the poet is in despair:

> My mouth doth water, and my breast doth swell,
> My tongue doth itch, my thoughts in labor be;
> Listen then, lordings, with good ear to me,
> For of my life I must a riddle tell.
> Toward Aurora's court a nymph doth dwell,
> Rich in all beauties which man's eye can see;
> Beauties so far from reach of words that we
> Abase her praise saying she doth excel;
> Rich in the treasure of deserved renown,
> Rich in the riches of a royal heart,
> Rich in those gifts which give th'eternal crown;
> Who, though most rich in these and every part
> Which make the patents of true worldly bliss,
> Hath no misfortune but that Rich she is.

The heavy playing on 'Rich' reveals Stella's identity as the
newly married Lady Rich. It was, significantly, one of the very
few sonnets suppressed in the first printing of 1591. Other
clues to the lovers' identities can be gleaned from sonnet 65,
where Astrophil asserts: 'Thou bear'st the arrow, I the arrow

head.' An arrow head was part of the Sidney coat of arms. There is also a reference to 'Penelope' in the fact that there are 108 sonnets, and 108 stanzas in the 11 songs that intersperse the sonnets. One hundred and eight was the number of Penelope's suitors in the *Odyssey*. Each sonnet, and each stanza, is a suitor standing in for the ever-importuning Astrophil.

As the sequence develops it becomes clear that even after Stella's marriage the poet lives in hope. She blushes when she sees him, as if guilty of a secret love (sonnet 66); she confesses her love for him, on the condition that it go no further (sonnet 69); the poet is in 'bliss' (sonnet 70); in the second song he finds her asleep and kisses her; she awakes, and is extremely cross. But by sonnet 81 she is fully conscious and kissing, though continuing to insist that it cannot be. This is the most compelling reason why *Astrophil and Stella* was never published in Philip's lifetime, and why the lovers' identities are concealed. Astrophil was kissing a married woman.

There is another way of looking at all this. Perhaps Philip never loved Penelope. In the twentieth century we all 'grew up' about *Astrophil and Stella*. Despite all the coded references to the lovers' identities, the sonnets were a self-conscious game with language and imagery, the fashionable discourse of a courtier-poet. The poet says and does all the things that are expected of the Petrarchan sonneteer. If it had not been Stella it would have been some other maiden. Critics have even speculated that *Astrophil and Stella* was a witty present to Stella on her bridal day, intended to point out the importance of virtue by presenting her with a fictitious, unvirtuous lover. Others have surmised that Philip may not have been interested in Penelope *until* her marriage, at which point he was stimulated to produce the sonnets, since a married, and therefore inaccessible, woman was required by the genre.

But if all Philip wanted was to praise some cool young woman in Petrarchan fashion, would he have gone to the lengths of inaugurating a new literary genre? It is tempting to feel that something more than a courtly game must have been fuelling this dazzling experiment. Stella was, as a matter of historical record, promised to Philip, and then given to someone else. We don't tend to dismiss Donne's or Shakespeare's love-sonnets as mere fantasies. Shouldn't we accord Sir Philip Sidney the same courtesy?

1 Another writer, Ernest Hemingway, received a similar war wound 332 years later: see chapter 35.

2 As reported in J.A. Symonds, *Sir Philip Sidney*: (1886), pp.174–5

3 A document exists to this effect signed by Edward Waterhouse, an agent of the Sidney family, of November 14, 1576.

5. THE TRAGICAL
HISTORY OF DR FAUSTUS
(c.1588)

One often hears of the 'Faust legend', as if the story of the pact-making necromancer were just that – a legend. But there was a real Faust, and one not too far distant in time from Christopher Marlowe. They might almost – *almost* – have met.

The contemporary references to the real Dr Faustus begin in 1507 with a letter from Johannes Tritheim, a humanist and physicist with a reputation as a magician, to his colleague the astrologer Johannes Virdung. It is a piece of gossip between two occultists:

> The man of whom you wrote me, George Sabellicus, who has presumed to call himself the prince of necromancers, is a vagabond, a babbler and a rogue, who deserves to be thrashed [. . .]. For what, other than symptoms of a very foolish and insane mind, are the titles assumed by this man, who shows himself to be a fool and not a philosopher? For thus he has formulated the title befitting him: Master George Sabellicus, the younger Faust, the chief of necromancers, astrologer, the second magus, palmist, diviner with earth and fire, second in the art of divination with water. Behold the foolish temerity of the man, the madness by which he is possessed [. . .] he ought to call himself a fool rather than a master.

This raises the possibility that there might have been two Fausts, a senior and a junior, but this is the only tantalizing reference to this idea. By 1513, one of these individuals – presumably the younger – had eclipsed the other and was making trouble at Erfurt. A letter of that year from Conrad Mutianus Rufus, canon of the Church of St Mary's at Gotha, to Heinrich Urbanus, a steward at the Cistercian cloister at Erfurt (Gotha and Erfurt are neighbouring towns), reads:

> Eight days ago there came to Erfurt a certain soothsayer by the name of George Faust, the demigod of Heidelberg, a mere braggart and fool. His claims, like those of all diviners, are idle and such physiognomy has no more weight than a water spider [. . .] I heard him babbling at an inn, but I did not reprove his boastfulness.

Fifteen years later, in the records of the City of Ingolstadt, we find another reference to George Faust of Heidelberg, who was 'ordered to leave the city and to spend his penny elsewhere' and 'not to take vengeance on or make fools of the authorities for this order'. In 1532 the city council of Nuremberg refused him safe conduct, reviling him as a 'great sodomite and necromancer'. In 1536 Joachim Camerarius (a teacher of Greek at Erfurt) wrote to Daniel Stibar (a councilman at Würzburg): 'I owe to your friend Faust the pleasure of discussing these affairs with you. I wish he had taught you something of this sort rather than puffed you up with the wind of silly superstition or held you in suspense with I know not what juggler's tricks.'

As a final proof that he was no mere piece of diabolical froth but a figure of some significance, he was mentioned in dispatches by both of the great figures of the German Reformation, Luther and Melanchthon. In Luther's *Table-Talk* of 1566 (published twenty years after Luther's death in 1546) there are two references, one of which is the following:

> Mention was made of magicians and the magic art, and how Satan blinded men. Much was said about Faust,

who called the devil his brother-in-law, and the remark was made: 'If I, Martin Luther, had given him even my hand, he would have destroyed me; but I would not have been afraid of him – with God as my protector, I would have given him my hand in the name of the Lord.'

Melanchthon, who may have met Faust,[1] wrote that Faust had tried to fly at Venice in the manner of Simon Magus, but had been dashed to the ground; and that at Vienna he had 'devoured another magician who was discovered a few days later in a certain cave'.

These are a few of the dozen or so contemporary references to Faust. If you had to sum them up they would point to a man who claimed occult powers, who was constantly at the centre of religious scandal (not a healthy place to be in the sixteenth century), who was an energetic self-publicist and widely travelled. But by 1540 the tales concerning his activities were beginning to shade towards the mythic. Many scholars give this year as a rough guess for the year of Faust's death.

In 1587 there was a major development in the story of Faust. The *Historia von D. Johann Fausten*, a book purporting to be a life of Faust, but spiced up with some previous tales of the devil-dealing of Simon Magus, Theophilus of Adana and others, and concentrating heavily on Faust's pact with Mephistopheles, was published in Germany. It was a Europe-wide best-seller. The earliest extant English translation, the full title of which is *The Historie of the damnable life, and deserved death of Doctor John Faustus*, also known as the *English Faust-book*, by the unknown 'P.F., Gent.', was printed 'at the little North doore of Paules, at the signe of the Gun', in 1592. This was Christopher Marlowe's chief source.[2]

The character of Doctor Faustus that Marlowe drew from the *English Faust-book* became one of the most influential in world literature.[3] Marlowe's Faustus is a man drunk with knowledge, at war with God for having made him a weak and mortal human, but aspiring none the less towards the super-human. Faustus thinks himself better informed than both God and the Devil ('Come, I think Hell's a fable'), but when he is cast into the pit realizes that all along he has been a mere pawn in the struggle of the eternal powers. His last-minute hedging and attempt to recant is one of the most moving episodes in Renaissance drama:

> Or let this hour be but
> A year, a month, a week, a natural day,
> That Faustus may repent and save his soul.
> *O lente, lente currite noctis equi!*
> The stars move still, time runs, the clock will strike.
> The devil will come, and Faustus must be damned.
> O, I'll leap up to my God: Who pulls me down?
> See, see, where Christ's blood streams in the firmament.

One of the eerie things about *The Tragical History of Doctor Faustus* is that the protagonist reminds us irresistibly of someone else: the author. After Marlowe's death in 1593, aged twenty-nine, in a tavern fight, Thomas Kyd said that Marlowe was prone to 'jest at the divine Scriptures, gibe at prayers, and strive in argument to frustrate and confute what hath been spoke or writ by prophets and such holy men.' An informer called Richard Baines said at Marlowe's inquest that 'almost into every company he cometh he persuades men to Atheism, willing them not to be afeared of bugbears and hobgoblins, and utterly scorning both God and his ministers.' Thomas Beard in 1597 said that he 'cursed and blasphemed to his last gasp, and together with his breath an oath flew out of his mouth.'

Unfortunately these accounts are inseparable from the politics of the time (the testimony of Thomas Kyd was extracted while he was imprisoned and in fear of his life). Even the grains of truth that they might contain could have been influenced by the reputation of the play (which was great). It is possible that Marlowe might have been in the habit of impersonating his own hero (as a joke?). So little is known about Christopher Marlowe. What sometimes pass as facts about his life – for example that he was homosexual – are based on the slenderest of evidence, and, in the absence of facts, a good deal of embroidering has gone on. Marlowe has become mythicized. In this he shares a great deal with that earlier figure, his almost-contemporary, the damnable Doctor Faustus.

1 According to a professor of Greek from Heidelberg, Augustin Lercheimer (1522–1603): 'The lewd, devilish fellow Faust stayed for a time in Wittenberg, as I stated before. He came at times to the house of Melanchthon, who gave him a good lecture, rebuked and warned him that he should reform in time, lest he come to an evil end, as finally happened.'
2 Scholarly consensus is that Marlowe worked from a slightly earlier English translation of the German *Historia* which is no longer extant, possibly of 1588, making it possible that Marlowe wrote the play in 1588/9. The first publication of the play was in 1604. His play is the first surviving dramatic treatment of the Faust story in any language, including German.
3 The Faust story, filtered through Marlowe, received later treatments by Lessing and Goethe.

6. HAMLET
(*c.*1600)

The legend of Hamlet dates to at least 400 years before Shakespeare. In around AD 1200 the Danish scholar Saxo Grammaticus (Saxo the Grammarian) wrote a history of the Danes which included the story of Amleth, a prince of Jutland. In the story Amleth's father Orvendil is joint ruler of Jutland with his brother Fengi, but Fengi, envious of Orvendil's success and covetous of Orvendil's wife Geruth, murders him and becomes sole king. Amleth feigns madness to avoid assassination, and finally and spectacularly revenges himself (he ties the drunken courtiers down as they sleep, sets fire to the palace, and runs Fengi through with his sword).

The tale was translated from its original Latin into French as part of François de Belleforest's *Histoires tragiques* in 1570, and made its first appearance in English in 1608. Shakespeare wrote *Hamlet* in around 1600, which means that the tale from Saxo would have been available to him only in French.

There was, however, another source, this time in English: a play, now lost, referred to in Shakespearian circles as the *ur-Hamlet*. It is often ascribed to Thomas Kyd, the author of *The Spanish Tragedy*. We know about this early 'Kydian' *Hamlet* through several contemporary references. The earliest is from the poet and pamphleteer Thomas Nashe,[1] and it occurs in his preface to Robert Greene's *Menaphon* (1589), where he writes satirically of his fellow hacks:

> It is a common practice now-a-days amongst a sort of shifting companions, that run through every art and thrive by none, to leave the trade of noverint[2] whereto

they were born and busy themselves with the endeavours of art, that could scarcely Latinize their neck-verse if they should have need; yet English Seneca read by candlelight yields many good sentences, as Blood is a beggar, and so forth, and if you entreat him fair in a frosty morning, he will afford you whole Hamlets, I should say handfuls, of tragical speeches. But O grief! *Tempus edax rerum*, what's that will last always? The sea exhaled by drops will in continuance be dry, and Seneca, let blood line by line and page by page, at length must needs die to our stage, which makes his famished followers to imitate the kid in Aesop, who, enamoured with the fox's newfangles, forsook all hopes of life to leap into a new occupation . . .

The 'kid in Aesop' has been taken as a punning reference to Thomas Kyd, and given the nearby reference to Seneca (Seneca was the antique model for the revenge tragedy, of which *The Spanish Tragedy* is the earliest Elizabethan example) this seems quite likely.

Two diaries also yield mention of the *ur-Hamlet*: the first is that of the theatrical impresario Philip Henslowe, who in 1594 recorded takings of 8 shillings for a performance of *Hamlet*. The second is that of the playwright Thomas Lodge, who wrote in 1596 of a character 'as pale as the Vizard of the ghost which cried so miserably at the theatre, like an oyster-wife, Hamlet, revenge!'

These, then, one surviving text and one lost, were Shakespeare's two known sources. He didn't add a great deal in plot terms: Saxo–Belleforest has the murder by an uncle, the marriage to a submissive widow, the ghost (only in Belle-forest[3]), Hamlet feigning madness, the trip to England accompanied by two courtiers, the letter ordering Hamlet's execution, the Ophelia-figure and the killing of a hidden spy.

The main elements that appear only in Shakespeare's version – but which themselves could have been taken from the *ur-Hamlet* – include the murder of Hamlet's father in secret (in Saxo–Belleforest everybody knows about it), the use of a play 'to catch the conscience of the king', and the death of Hamlet in the mêlée that ends the play.

Such is the general state of scholarship on the sources for *Hamlet*. But an odd little fact exists. Shakespeare had a son called Hamnet – Hamnet, with an 'n'. 'Hamnet' and 'Hamlet' are so close that Shakespeare must surely either have named his son after his play, or his play after his son. Hamnet was born in 1585, and *Hamlet* was written fifteen years later in 1600, and so the obvious conclusion is that it must have been the latter. However, complications immediately arise. Hamnet and his twin sister Judith were named after Shakespeare's neighbours in Stratford, Hamnet and Judith Sadler. The spellings 'Hamnet' and 'Hamlet' seem to have been interchangeable in the records of the period: Hamnet Sadler was also recorded as Hamlet Sadler.

Shakespeare's son Hamnet died, aged eleven, in 1596. This was four years before Shakespeare came to write *Hamlet*.

What does this mean? There are several theories concerning the influence of Hamnet on *Hamlet*. The first is that father and son were not particularly close (Shakespeare spent all of Hamnet's life away in London) and that the story of the Danish prince was just a random subject for a revenge tragedy: Hamnet was not in his mind.[4] A second theory has Shakespeare turning to the Hamlet legend as a way of exploring his grief over the death of his son. This idea has recently been given a new spin by the critic Stephen Greenblatt, who has pointed out that certain strange features of *Hamlet* – particularly Hamlet's protracted indecision about whether or not to act on the ghost's advice – exist because Shakespeare wished to draw attention to the changeover from Catholic to Protestant burial rites, a changeover he had recently witnessed at his son's graveside.[5]

A third theory, however, gives Shakespeare as the author – or co-author – of the *ur-Hamlet*.[6] This has several strong points. The chief suspect for the author of an early version of a famous play must be, in the absence of any convincing evidence to the contrary, the author of the famous play himself. The punning 'kid in Aesop' in Nashe would simply refer to Kyd as the most prominent English follower of Seneca, and not finger him as the author of the *ur-Hamlet*. The references in Henslowe and Lodge would be to a lost play by Shakespeare himself (and, possibly, A.N. Other) called *Hamlet*. The dates for Hamnet's birth now fit. Hamnet was born in 1585, and the *ur-Hamlet*t was written some time in the mid-1580s (by the evidence of Nashe). In this scheme of things, the choice of the Hamlet-legend as a subject for a play would have been made at the same time as Shakespeare named Hamnet after his neighbour. It would have been a christening-present.

It is an intriguing possibility. Shakespeare was twenty-one years old in 1585, just at the beginning of his playwrighting career. If he did indeed write his first *Hamlet* in that year, in a spirit of celebration at the birth, and perhaps with a happy ending – Saxo and Belleforest both have happy endings – it would probably not have occurred to him that in fifteen years' time he would feel compelled to revisit the play with a new, darker understanding of the bond between a father and a son.

1 Nashe (1567–c.1600) was a jobbing controversialist with a florid style who also wrote an early, unauthorized preface to Sir Philip Sidney's *Astrophil and Stella*: see chapter 4.
2 A loose term for a lawyer.

3 Belleforest's work was more than a straight translation – he expanded the tale to twice its original length and added details, among them the ghost ('*les ombres de Horvvendille*').

4 The fact that Shakespeare wrote several comedies shortly after the death of Hamnet – *Much Ado About Nothing*, *As You Like It*, *The Merry Wives of Windsor* – is sometimes cited in support of the theory that Shakespeare was not particularly affected by his son's death.

5 See *Hamlet in Purgatory* (2001) and *Will in the World: How Shakespeare became Shakespeare* (2004). This controversial theory hinges on the idea that the innovative 'inwardness' in the characterization of Prince Hamlet is due to the fact that Hamlet is uncertain whether the ghost is a bona fide spirit from Purgatory (a Catholic way of looking at it) or a devil sent to tempt him (a Protestant way of looking at it). This reflected Shakespeare's – and England's – sense of ambivalence about the prohibition of Catholic funerary rites, which enabled the living to intercede for Purgatory-bound souls.

6 Shakespeare's authorship of the *ur-Hamlet* has been advanced by a number of scholars, including the critic and Shakespeare biographer Harold Bloom: see his *Shakespeare: The Invention of the Human* (1998). That Shakespeare occasionally collaborated is beyond doubt: he worked with John Fletcher on *The Two Noble Kinsmen*, and other possible collaborators on various plays include Thomas Middleton, George Wilkins and George Peele.

7. THE DUCHESS OF MALFI
(c.1614)

Amalfi is a seaside town in the south-west of Italy, its beach-front crammed with hotels, restaurants and coloured umbrellas. In medieval times it was the capital of the small Duchy of Amalfi, dominated by Naples a few miles to the north.

In 1490, Alfonso Piccolomini, a member of one of Amalfi's ruling families, married the noblewoman Giovanna d'Aragona. She was twelve years old (see chapter 43). Alfonso became the Duke of Amalfi three years later in 1493, making Giovanna the Duchess of Amalfi. In 1498 Alfonso died, and Giovanna, now twenty, and with an infant son, was left in sole charge. Then things started to go wrong.

Giovanna had two powerful brothers: Carlo, Marquis of Gerace, and Lodovico, Cardinal of Santa Maria in Cosmedin. Their main concern after the death of Alfonso was to control her remarriage so as to strengthen their own political influence. But the Duchess had other ideas. Around 1505 she began an affair with the major-domo of her household, Antonio Bologna, and later married him in secret. Over the next couple of years she bore him two children. By the time of her third pregnancy, her brothers had got wind of the scandal, and in 1510, the lovers, with the two children and the new baby, decided to flee.

On the pretext of going to Loreto on pilgrimage, they travelled to Ancona, but there they were overtaken by agents of the brothers. The Duchess and her two youngest children were brought back to Amalfi and imprisoned. Antonio escaped with the eldest son but was later murdered in Milan. The Duchess and her children then disappeared from history. Her first son, from her first marriage, became ruler of Amalfi in her place.

Such are the historical facts. The next contributor to the tale of the Duchess was one Matteo Bandello, an Italian monk, diplomat, soldier and writer, whose *Novelle* were published between 1554 and 1573. The *Novelle* were collections of stories of racy goings-on at Renaissance courts, in the manner of Boccaccio's *Decameron*. One of the tales was entitled '*Il signor Antonio Bologna sposa la duchessa d'Amalfi, e tutti due sono ammazzati*' (Antonio Bologna marries the Duchess of Amalfi and they are both killed). Bandello may have known Antonio, perhaps even witnessed his murder, and he very likely inserted himself into the narrative in the character of Delio. From Bandello's account we get a number of important additional details, among them the first appearance of the character of Daniele da Bozolo, Antonio's assassin (later very important to the Webster play as the hired killer Bosola) and the strangling of the Duchess and her children.

At this point matters moved a little closer to home. Many people will have wondered why Elizabethan and Jacobean drama is obsessed with happenings in Spain and Italy. The answer lies substantially with one man: William Painter. In 1566 he published *The Palace of Pleasure*, a collection of translations into English of tales from Boccaccio's *Decameron*, Marguerite of Navarre's *Heptameron* and Bandello's *Novelle*, mediated through the French of François de Belleforest. The tales – including, of course, that of the Duchess – were immensely popular. Shakespeare certainly read *The Palace of Pleasure* (its influence is seen in *All's Well That Ends Well*, *Romeo and Juliet* and *Timon of Athens*), as did Beaumont and Fletcher, Massinger, Marston and Webster. The Italy–Spain hybrid that they derived from Painter, with its incense-heavy Catholic exoticism, was the backdrop to a new form of theatre: revenge tragedy. Revenge tragedy derived ultimately from Seneca, but its scenery was Painter. It dealt with conflicts within or between families, set in motion by ambitious malcontents, and culminating in the shedding of blood, much blood; sometimes the blood of the entire cast, as in one of the greatest of all revenge tragedies, *The Duchess of Malfi*.

Webster, in trying to spice Painter up (and Painter was already pretty lurid), added yet more detail. The Duchess's brother Ferdinand (Webster's name for Carlo) is portrayed as not just a revenger but a slavering psychopath, proposing to stew his sister's baby and feed it to its father:

> I would have their bodies
> Burn't in a coale-pit, with the ventage stop'd,
> That their curs'd smoake might not ascend to Heaven:
> Or dippe the sheetes they lie in, in pitch or sulphure,
> Wrap them in't, and then light them like a match:
> Or else to boile their Bastard to a cullisse,
> And give't his leacherous father, to renew
> The sinne of his backe.

Webster devoted all of Act Four to the psychological torture of the Duchess in prison by Ferdinand. In his attempt to drive her mad Ferdinand pretends to forgive her and gives her his hand to kiss, but she discovers in horror that it is the severed hand of a dead man. He puts wax figures of a dead Antonio and their dead children into the cell. He brings capering lunatics to shriek into her ears. Such scenes led later commentators to feel that Webster was all rather too much: Rupert Brooke wrote that Webster was 'full of the feverish and ghastly turmoil of a nest of maggots'. And, as is compulsory in revenge tragedy, the body count rises inexorably. The Duchess and her chambermaid are strangled, Antonio is slain in the street, and in the final eruption of violence the entire *dramatis personae* are slaughtered, including the two brothers and Bosola. No major character is left standing. The effect is almost comic, rather like the end of *Reservoir Dogs*.

Webster was thus handed his title by history. The transformation from *d'Amalfi* to 'of Malfi' is easy to see. *La Duchessa d'Amalfi* in Italian became *La Duchesse d'Amalfi* in the French of Belleforest: *d'Amalfi* was mistaken for *de Malfi*, and translated into English as 'of Malfi'.

However his choice of the story of the Duchess may have had other motives.

The tale had striking parallels with happenings in Jacobean England. Lady Arabella Stuart, whose uncle was Lord Darnley (the second husband of Mary, Queen of Scots), had been forbidden by James I to marry, because her (potentially Catholic) children would have had a claim to the throne. In 1610 she secretly married, then eloped with William Seymour, Duke of Somerset. Dressing (in good dramaturgical fashion) as a man, she escaped halfway across the Channel before being intercepted by the King's agents. She was brought back to the Tower and imprisoned for life, dying in 1615. Arabella was thus still alive, and imprisoned close by, when *The Duchess of Malfi* was first performed – by the troupe known as the King's Men.

So although *The Duchess of Malfi* had its origins in a century-old Italian story, Webster knew that the subject of his play, and its mix of star-crossed love, Catholic intrigue and false imprisonment, would put the audience in mind of a much more recent English duchess. It is not difficult to see where Webster's satiric sympathies lay. He treats the character of the Italian duchess in a much more sympathetic light than Painter (who is moralistic and condemnatory of her marriage), and makes the pursuing brothers into lycanthropic monsters. *The Duchess of Malfi*, it turns out, is about not only a long-dead Renaissance princess, but also the highly topical machinations of Jacobean power-politics.

8. THE TENTH MUSE LATELY SPRUNG UP IN AMERICA
(1650)

Traditionally, there are nine muses: Calliope (the muse of epic poetry), Clio (the muse of history), Erato (the muse of erotic poetry), Terpsichore (the muse of dance), Melpomene (the muse of tragedy), Polyhymnia (the muse of sacred song), Euterpe (the muse of ordinary song), Thalia (the muse of comedy and pastoral poetry) and Urania (the muse of astronomy). The muses are, naturally, deities, not flesh and blood women. They symbolize the arts and inspire artistic creation, and are invoked by male artists with a deadline: Homer, Virgil, Shakespeare ('O for a muse of fire'), Milton or Robert Graves. When a living woman is styled the 'tenth muse' there must always be some sense of irony. A real woman can never be a goddess. Except, perhaps, if you are Robert Graves.

Nevertheless a number of real women have been put forward as the tenth muse. They have included Sappho, the French poet Antoinette de la Garde Deshoulières, the French novelist Madeleine de Scudéry, Queen Christina of Sweden, the Spanish poet and writer Sor Juana Inés de la Cruz, and the English writer and dramatist Hannah More. Interestingly, all of these post-Sappho tenth muses (apart from Hannah More, 1745–1833) lived in the seventeenth century, as did the most famous of all tenth muses, Anne Bradstreet. It seems that the sobriquet was a piece of seventeenth-century publishers' hype. It is unlikely that any of the women chose it. Anne Bradstreet certainly did not: as a Puritan wife and mother she would have been quite disturbed to find herself in the company of Sappho.

Anne Bradstreet's book was *The Tenth Muse Lately Sprung Up in America*. It had an unusual genesis. Anne was among the

Nonconformist English refugees of the 'Great Migration' to New England in 1630. These were the early years of the American colonial experiment: the so-called Pilgrim Fathers had settled on the east coast only ten years earlier. When Anne's party landed at Charlestown, Massachusetts, after a gruelling 72-day voyage, they found a colony ravaged by sickness and hunger. Her father wrote: 'We found the colony in a sad and unexpected condition, above eight of them being dead the winter before; and many of those alive, weak and sick [...] We found ourselves wholly unable to feed them.' Anne and her family were forced to scrape a living from the land, eating 'clams and museles and ground nuts and acorns', probably living for months in teepees. After several years of struggle they moved to Merrimack (later North Andover), where Anne gave birth to seven of her eight children. Somehow she also found time to write. By 1647 she had amassed a collection of work that seems to have circulated among her relatives: in that year her brother-in-law, the Reverend John Woodbridge, sailed to England carrying with him several of her poems. Without her permission he arranged for their publication in 1650 in London 'at the signe of the Bible in Popes Head-Alley'. This was the volume dubbed *The Tenth Muse*, a title that was simply tacked on to the poems. With it she became the first published poet, male or female, in colonial America.

The full title of the book, as it appeared in the lavish manner of the seventeenth century, was *The Tenth Muse Lately sprung up in AMERICA. OR Severall Poems, compiled with great variety of Wit and Learning, full of delight. Wherein is contained a compleat discourse and description of the Four Elements, Constitutions, Ages of Man* [and] *Seasons of the Year. Together with an Exact Epitomie of the Four Monarchies, viz The Assyrian, Persian, Grecian* [and] *Roman. Also a Dialogue between Old England and New, concerning the late troubles. With divers other pleasant and serious Poems. By a gentle-*

woman in those parts. Anne was not named on the title page, though her identity was revealed in a commendatory note as 'Mistris *Anne Bradstreet*, Vertue's true and lively Patterne [...] At present residing in the Occidentall parts of the World, in *America*, alias *NOV-ANGLIA*'. An introduction from her brother-in-law recommended her 'gracious demeanour, her eminent parts, her pious conversation, her courteous disposition, her exact diligence in her place, and discreet managing of her Family occasions'. He added: 'I fear the displeasure of no person in the publishing of these Poems but the Author, without whose knowledge, and contrary to her expectation, I have presumed to bring to publick view, what she resolved in such a manner should never see the Sun.' He was right to fear Anne's displeasure. On seeing her new-minted book she recorded her feelings in one of her best-known poems, 'The Author to her Book' (included in the second edition of 1678):

> Thou ill-form'd offspring of my feeble brain,
> Who after birth did'st by my side remain,
> Till snatcht from thence by friends, less wise than true,
> Who thee abroad, expos'd to publick view;
> Made thee in raggs, halting to th' press to trudg,
> Where errors were not lessened (all may judg) . . .

But *The Tenth Muse* was a great success.[1] The idea that a woman, fighting savages with one hand and bearing children with the other, had had time to write a book of poetry, caused a sensation. Perhaps when the first moon-based poet publishes a collection there will be a similar éclat.

The poems themselves now make dull reading. It is difficult to say whether they did then: they certainly sold well. They were chiefly rambling treatments of traditional themes (the four humours, the monarchs of the ancient world) after the style of a forgotten epic poet, Guillaume Du Bartas. It was only in the 1678 and subsequent editions that her smaller, domestic poems were included. These poems, far from the style of Du Bartas, speak of a growing poetic independence and maturity. Their titles alone vividly communicate the realities of pioneer life: 'Upon the burning of our house, July 10th, 1666', 'Upon some distemper of body', 'Upon my Daughter Hannah Wiggin her recovery from a dangerous feaver', 'On my dear Grand-child Simon Bradstreet, Who dyed on 16. Novemb. 1669. being but a moneth, and one day old'. These are the poems that now appear in anthologies, and for which Anne Bradstreet will be remembered. In these the reader glimpses things personal, sometimes shocking: experiences of bodily pain unrelieved by medicine, struggles with unbelief in the face of terrible loss, love of God in spite of all, hope for heavenly reward. Tender lyrics such as 'To my Dear and loving Husband' are a world away from the bombastic and unchosen title *The Tenth Muse Lately Sprung Up in America*:

> If ever two were one, then surely we.
> If ever man were lov'd by wife, then thee;
> If ever wife was happy in a man,
> Compare with me ye women, if you can.
> I prize thy love more than whole Mines of gold
> Or all the riches that the East doth hold.
> My love is such that Rivers cannot quench,
> Nor ought but love from thee, give recompence.
> Thy love is such I can no way repay,
> The heavens reward thee manifold I pray.
> Then while we live, in love lets so persever
> That when we live no more, we may live ever.

1 Anne edited the second edition, which was published posthumously in 1678.

9. CINDERELLA, OR THE LITTLE GLASS SLIPPER
(1697)

The first major survey of Cinderellas was in 1893, when Marian Roalfe Cox gathered some 345 versions of the tale, mainly from oral sources in Europe. By the 1950s the number had risen to around 700. Then in the 1960s and 1970s numerous extra-European Cinderellas began to emerge: Cinderellas from Java, China, pre-Columbian America, Africa and elsewhere. Analysis of story motifs allows folklorists to place any story in a 'tale-type' index, the best known of which is the Aarne–Thompson index.[1] Cinderella is Aarne–Thompson 510A (girl is ill-treated and recognized by means of shoe).

The first Cinderella, by this somewhat scaled-down plot-line, is Rhodopis, an Egyptian girl in a tale first collected by Strabo in the first century BC. Rhodopis, while bathing in the Nile, has her slipper stolen by an eagle, who takes it to the king at Memphis: the king falls in love with the shoe, seeks its owner and marries her. No pumpkin coach or mice footmen, but some distinct similarities. In the ninth century, in China, more familiar motifs start to appear. In the Chinese Cinderella a girl is ill-treated by a stepmother and stepsisters, given a magical cloak, is seen by a prince who falls in love with her, loses a slipper, is identified by it, and marries the prince. This written version antedates European written versions by 700 years. Whether there are lines of influence between the two traditions is unknown, but the circumstantial evidence is compelling. And a Chinese origin for 'a tale of small feet' seems to make sense.

The version of Cinderella that most readers will be familiar with first appeared as '*Cendrillon, ou la petite pantoufle de verre*', one of the stories in Charles Perrault's *Contes de ma mère l'Oye* (*Mother Goose Tales*) in 1697. His immediate written source was '*La Gatta Cenerentola*' from Giambattista Basile's *Pentamerone* of 1634. Cenerentola comes ultimately from *cinis*, ash, and *tollere*, to carry: thus the heroine is an ash-carrier, or ash-girl. In Perrault the sisters refer to her unkindly as Cucendron – ash-bottom, or ash-arse: this found its way into the first English translation as Cinder-breech.[2] Perrault has all the paraphernalia we recognize from Disney: the fairy godmother, the pumpkin coach, the glass slippers, the rat coachman, and so on.

It is the detail of the little glass slipper that brings Perrault's title into an area of controversy. The glass slipper was his own addition (it does not appear in Basile, where the shoe is merely 'the richest and prettiest patten you could imagine'), and he gives it star billing – 'Cinderella, or the Little Glass Slipper'. Before modern industrial toughening, glass would have been an entirely impractical, not to say lethal, material for slippers, and appears in very few other Cinderella stories. It has been suggested that Perrault drew on oral sources in which the slipper was made of *vair*, an archaic French word for an ermine-like fur, and changed it to *verre*, or glass, either because he liked the sound of it or out of a genuine error, and thus the tale was altered for ever. One of the earliest champions of this theory was Balzac, in his *Études Philosophiques sur Catherine de Médicis* (1836), but its spread was guaranteed when it was taken up by encyclopedias such as the *Encyclopedia Britannica*. Among the most recent encyclopedias to cite the theory uncritically is the fourth edition of Benét's *Reader's Encyclopedia* of 1996. Folklorists still occasionally cite the *vair/verre* hypothesis as fact.[3] But it is almost certainly false. The reasons were pointed out by the folklorist Paul Delarue in a short essay in *Le Monde* in 1951.

Essentially, the *vair/verre* hypothesis depends on the idea that glass is very uncommon as a slipper-material in other tales of the Cinderella cycle, and that any other traditions which do contain glass slippers can be seen as deriving from Perrault. But Delarue pointed out that while there are only a few Cinderella tales with glass slippers, motif-analysis of these tales does not bear out the assertion that they are necessarily derivative. A Scottish version of Cinderella which includes glass shoes also includes the 'helpful animal motif', which, for folklorists, sets heads nodding. Animals helping the heroine in Cinderella stories – frogs (Africa), fish (China) and giant crabs (Java) – indicate antiquity, and in the Scottish tale it is a little black lamb, not a fairy, who dispenses the rich raiment that enables Cinderella to attract the prince.

Delarue deals his knockout blow by finding this dangerous item of footwear in *other* antique tales. In a Gaelic story a heroine who desires to climb a glass mountain in order to find her husband must wear glass shoes. In an Irish tale it is the hero who wears glass shoes when rescuing a princess from a sea serpent; with a satisfying role reversal, when he drops his own shoe it is she who uses it as an aid to recognize him. The point here is that glass is a magical material, on a par with diamond and gold (all of which are materials for objects, including shoes, in fairy tales). Thus in various stories we have a glass mountain, a boat of glass, a castle of glass, a tree with leaves of glass; there is even a story of a giant with a beard of glass (as well as a giant with a beard of copper and a giant with a beard of gold). Impossible things are permissible in the magical world, and a beard of glass is as impractical as shoes of glass. The fact that glass is likely to shatter, and that fur would be more sensible, is an absurd attempt to judge the fairy-tale world by the standards of our own mundane one.

Perhaps the debate will never be resolved to everyone's satisfaction, but the fact remains that the original story with the fur has never been located. The *verre/vair* hypothesis has itself become a story. It is certainly neat, and useful to trot out at parties. And perhaps there are other reasons why it is so persistent.

The insistence on *fur,* as the critic Alan Dundes has pointed out, may be the clue. Shoes are associated with female sexuality and marriage in many traditions. The shoe is designed to fit and enclose a foot: it is a metaphor. In Britain we still throw shoes after a retreating bridal car, and in some Chinese traditions a bride gives a gift of shoes to her husband. Glass too has a sexual significance, this time to do with female virginity: in the Jewish marriage ceremony the groom crushes a glass to seal the marriage contract.[4] The symbolism is obvious. But for the persistent encylopedists and their urban-myth internet followers, the subtle and restrained symbolism of shoes and glass, in the context of sex, betrothal and marriage, is not good enough. No, they must have fur. Obviouser and obviouser. Interpreters and explicators, unconsciously it seems, themselves become storytellers.

1 The Aarne–Thompson Index, first published in 1910, lists 2,500 basic plots from around the world.
2 Here we get a glimpse of the vernacular Cinderella which those of us brought up on Disney find rather revolting. Cinderella tales are often distinguished by their violence. In the Grimm brothers' *Aschenputtel* (1812), one of the wicked sisters, in an attempt to fit into the shoe, cuts off her toes; the other slices off her heel. The prince (a trustful soul) only suspects something when he sees blood oozing out on to the floor of his carriage. For their reward, the sisters have their eyes pecked out by birds.
3 See, for example, Jane Yolen, 'America's Cinderella' in *Children's Literature in Education*, 8 (1977)
4 And where does he crush it? Under his shoe.

10. THE RAPE OF THE LOCK
(1712)

Some time early in 1712, the 7th Lord Petre committed a gallant little rape. At a social gathering, perhaps a ball or card party, he furtively snipped a lock of hair from the head of a young beauty, Arabella Fermor, and carried it off as a trophy. The Fermors and the Petres, two prominent Catholic families, stopped talking to one another, and Alexander Pope (another Catholic) was brought in, a poetic troubleshooter, to defuse the tension. This he did with the mock epic *The Rape of the Lock*, a poem intended to 'make a jest of it, and laugh them together again'. It apparently achieved its object, since Arabella Fermor 'took it so well as to give about copies of it' and later posed for a portrait in which she was shown wearing a prominent crucifix necklace, one specifically described in the poem.[1] But the poem did not achieve the ultimate reconciliation, the marriage of Arabella and Lord Petre. In a matter of months Petre was married to someone else.

In the poem, Arabella appears as 'Belinda'[2] (Arabella – Bella – Belinda) and Lord Petre is cast as 'the Baron'. Canto I sees Belinda at her dressing table; in Canto II she makes a pleasure cruise on the Thames (a joking reference to the sea voyages of heroic poetry); Canto III is set in Hampton Court, where the barbering offence takes place; and Cantos IV and V are focused on a skirmish between the nymphs and fops, and the ascent of the lock to heaven, where it becomes a comet (comet, from *kometes*, 'long-haired'):

> But trust the Muse – she saw it upward rise,
> Tho' mark'd by none but quick, poetic eyes: [. . .]
> A sudden Star, it shot thro' liquid air,
> And drew behind a radiant trail of hair.

The style is that of the mock heroic, in which trivial actions are magnified as if they were the doings of gods or heroes. It was a standard vehicle for satire, used in Dryden's *MacFlecknoe*, Samuel Garth's *The Dispensary*, Boileau's *Le Lutrin* and other works, all of which Pope knew well. Mock-heroic effects depended heavily on knowledge of the ultimate fount, the Latin verses of Homer and Virgil. Echoes of the *Iliad* or the *Aeneid* are everywhere in *The Rape of the Lock*, and Pope was later the acclaimed translator of both the *Iliad* and the *Odyssey*.

The work which almost certainly influenced the choice of title was Alessandro Tassoni's mock-epic *The Rape of the Bucket*, from 1622. ('Rape' in both poems was ultimately from *rapere*, to steal or snatch, and did not have a primarily sexual signification.) In this piece of scholarly ludicrousness, two Italian towns, Modena and Bologna, go to war with one another over the theft of a bucket from a well. The gods take sides in the struggle, sometimes rather ridiculously. Saturn travels to the celestial parliament sitting on a chamber pot, and Juno is unavailable because she is having her hair cut. Tassoni makes his purposes clear in the second stanza:

> *vedrai, s'al cantar mio porgi l'orecchia,*
> *Elena trasformarsi in una Secchia.*

> You will see, if you bend your ear to my song,
> Helen transformed into a Bucket.

The Rape of the Bucket was a best-seller in Italy and was known Europe-wide, and while Pope could have read it in Italian, he probably encountered it in English. A translation of the first part of Tassoni's poem appeared in 1710, two years before the composition of *The Rape of the Lock*. 'Done from the Italian into English Rhime', it was the work of John Ozell, one of the powerhouses of English translation in the early eighteenth century, the man responsible for English editions of Molière, Racine, Cervantes, Corneille and many others. In 1712 he produced an important edition of the *Iliad*, which Pope drew on in his own translation.

But Mr Pope and Mr Ozell were not on very good terms. Ozell had attacked William Wycherley, a friend of Pope's, and by doing so had drawn the wrath of the Scriblerians (Ozell was also satirized by Swift). In 1708 Pope caricatured Ozell as the very model of a time-serving literary hack:

> Reviving Perrault, murdering Boileau, he
> Slander'd the ancients first, then Wycherley;
> Which yet not much that old bard's anger raised,
> Since those were slander'd most whom Ozell praised.

Things went from bad to worse. Ozell was one of the fools mentioned by name in the *Dunciad* of 1729:

> How, with less reading than makes felons 'scape,
> Less human genius than God gives an ape,
> Small thanks to France, and none to Rome or Greece,
> A past, vamp'd, future, old, revived, new piece,
> 'Twixt Plautus, Fletcher, Shakspeare, and Corneille,
> Can make a Cibber, Tibbald, or Ozell.

That same year Ozell decided to bite back, as reported by Theophilus Cibber (son of Colley) in 1753:

> Ozell was incensed to the last degree by this usage, and in a paper called *The Weekly Medley*, September 1729, he published the following strange Advertisement. 'As to my learning, this envious wretch knew, and every body knows, that the whole bench of bishops, not long ago, were pleased to give me a purse of guineas for discovering the erroneous

translations of the Common Prayer in Portugueze, Spanish, French, Italian, &c. As for my genius, let Mr. Cleland shew better verses in all Pope's works, than Ozell's version of Boileau's *Lutrin*, which the late lord Hallifax was so well pleased with, that he complimented him with leave to dedicate it to him, &c. &c. Let him shew better and truer poetry in *The Rape of the Lock*, than in Ozell's *Rape of the Bucket*, which, because an ingenious author happened to mention in the same breath with Pope's, viz.

"Let Ozell sing the Bucket, Pope the Lock",

the little gentleman[3] had like to have run mad; and Mr. Toland and Mr. Gildon publicly declared Ozell's Translation of Homer to be, as it was prior, so likewise superior, to Pope's.

The wars between the singer of the Bucket and the singer of the Lock seem as fevered and ridiculous as the battles between Modena and Bologna or the nymphs and fops of Hampton Court. One asks oneself why Pope was so angry with Ozell. An obvious answer presents itself. Ozell had committed the unpardonable sin of helping Pope write his best-known poem.

1 'On her white breast a sparkling Cross she wore/Which Jews might kiss, and Infidels adore.'

2 Belinda appears in the epigraph to the poem, from Martial: '*Nolueram, Belinda, tuos violare capillos; Sedjuvat, hoc precibus me tribuisse tuis,*' (I was unwilling, Belinda, to ravish your locks; but I rejoice to have answered your prayers.) 'Belinda', however, was Pope's interpolation: in the original Latin of Martial the addressee is 'Polytimus'. Martial was the ancient world's foremost author of the obscene epigram, and Polytimus is described elsewhere in Martial's epigrams as 'very lecherous on women'. This is one among many bawdy references in *The Rape of the Lock*.

3 The 'little gentleman' was of course Pope, who never reached a greater height than 4 feet 6 inches.

11. SHAMELA
(1741)

The title page of *Shamela* reads:

AN
APOLOGY
FOR THE
LIFE
OF
Mrs. SHAMELA ANDREWS.
In which, the many notorious FALSHOODS and MIS-
REPRSENTATIONS of a Book called
PAMELA,
Are exposed and refuted; and all the matchless ARTS of that
young Politician, set in a true and just Light.
Together with
A full Account of all that passed between her and Parson
Arthur Williams; whose Character is represented in a manner
something different from what he bears in *PAMELA*. The
whole being exact Copies of authentick Papers delivered to
the Editor.
Necessary to be had in all FAMILIES.
By Mr. *CONNY KEYBER*.

From this rococo beginning it can be seen that Fielding's main target was *Pamela*, Samuel Richardson's smash-hit novel of 1740. The plot of *Pamela* is fairly simple: the heroine is a maid in the service of Mr B., who tries repeatedly to seduce her. Pamela foils all attempts on her virtue until Mr B., frustrated beyond endurance, makes a marriage proposal, which she accepts. The End. The subtitle of *Pamela*, *Virtue*

Rewarded, leaves no doubt about the high moral tone of the book. Some, however, detected a whiff of hypocrisy. Richardson claimed that he had excluded anything 'inflammatory' in the book – that it was intended merely as a conduct manual for young ladies – but *Pamela*, which is basically a tease spread over 800 pages, has a force-nine erotic charge. Almost as soon as it left the presses *Pamela* had drawn mockery and parody in a genre of books now known as 'anti-Pamelas',[1] and Fielding was first off the blocks with *Shamela*, published only five months after the book that had inspired it.

Shamela is a splendidly immoral little squib, the story of a faux-naïve strumpet on the make, out to ensnare Squire Booby (the counterpart of Mr B.), all the while carrying on an affair with Parson Williams. *Shamela* parodies *Pamela* on a formal and textual level, reversing its moral basis but at the same time oddly paralleling it, as if *Shamela* presented the 'real' thoughts of Pamela. It is very funny:

O Madam, I have strange Things to tell you! As I was reading in that charming Book about the Dealings, in comes my Master – to be sure he is a precious One. *Pamela,* says he, what Book is that, I warrant you *Rochester's* Poems. – No, forsooth, says I, as pertly as I could; why how now Saucy Chops, Boldface, says he – Mighty pretty Words, says I, pert again. – Yes (says he) you are a d–d, impudent, stinking, cursed, confounded jade, and I have a great Mind to kick your A –. You kiss – says I. A-gad, says he, and so I will; with that he caught me in his Arms, and kissed me till he made my Face all over Fire. Now this served purely you know, to put upon the Fool for Anger. O! What precious Fools Men are! And so I flung from him in a mighty Rage, and pretended as how I would go out at the Door; but when I came to the End of the Room, I stood still, and my Master cryed

out, Hussy, Slut, Saucebox, Boldface, come hither – Yes
to be sure, says I; why don't you come, says he; what
should I come for, says I; if you don't come to me, I'll
come to you, says he; I shan't come to you I assure you,
says I. Upon which he run up, caught me in his Arms,
and flung me upon a Chair, and began to offer to touch
my Under-Petticoat. Sir, says I, you had better not offer
to be rude; well, says he, no more I won't then; and away
he went out of the Room. I was so mad to be sure I could
have cry'd.

One feels sorry for Squire Booby: despite this setback,
Shamela soon outmanoeuvres him, and once the wedding is
over cuckolds and half-bankrupts him.

But *Pamela* was not the only target of *Shamela*. The full
title, *An Apology for the Life of Mrs Shamela Andrews*, and
its pseudonymous authorship by one 'Conny Keyber' reveals
a second mark. Colley Cibber was the poet laureate, an
appointee of the Whig ministry of Robert Walpole, and much
scorned as an establishment propagandist by his rivals,
notably Alexander Pope, who made him the hero of the
Dunciad. Cibber's vainglorious memoirs of 1740 were
entitled *An Apology for the Life of Mr Colley Cibber*. The
transformation from 'Colley Cibber' to 'Conny Keyber' was
in reference to Cibber's Danish ancestry: he was regularly
ridiculed in the press as 'Minheer Keiber'. ('Conny',
originally meaning a rabbit, was slang for the dupe of a thief
or trickster.) The feud between Cibber and Fielding went back
to the early 1730s, when Fielding was a struggling playwright
and Cibber the manager of the Drury Lane Theatre. Fielding
had attacked Cibber in *The Author's Farce* (1730), and
Cibber, in his *Apology*, had represented Fielding as a hack
and a failure. The title page of *Shamela* was an attempt to
mock the *Apology*, and in the long introduction to *Shamela*,

written in the form of various dedicatory and commendatory letters, there were many little anti-Cibber and anti-Walpole touches.

Shamela was an overnight success and marked an important career change for Fielding. He had spent his youth writing plays: *Shamela* was his first novel. It was quickly followed, in 1742, by *Joseph Andrews*, the story of the brother of Shamela, and then in 1743 *Jonathan Wild* (another anti-Walpole production). In 1749 he produced his greatest novel, *Tom Jones*.

One postscript is of some interest. Three years after the death of his wife Charlotte in 1744, Fielding married, not without scandal, his wife's maid Mary Daniel, who was six months pregnant at the time. One wonders if he had *Shamela* – or alternatively *Pamela* – in mind.

1 After Eliza Haywood's *Anti-Pamela, or Feign'd Innocence Detected* of 1741.

12. FANNY HILL
(1748/9)

As soon as I had closed the door, I said, 'Old fellow, did you ever see *Fanny Hill*, a beautiful book of love and pleasure?'

'What, a smutty book, I suppose you mean? No, Walter, but if you have got it I should wonderfully like to look at it,' he said, his eyes sparkling with animation.

'Here it is, my boy, only I hope it won't excite you too much; you can look it over by yourself, as I read the *Times*,' said I, taking it out of my dressing-case, and handing it to his eager grasp.

The Pearl magazine, August 1879

Fanny Hill is John Cleland's picaresque tale of sexual initiation and adventure set in the brothels and byways of mid-eighteenth-century England. It is *Moll Flanders* with the dirty bits left in; or, if you prefer, *Pamela* with the clean bits left out.

Fanny Hill is a pun, that much seems clear. Or two puns. The surname Hill is a reference to the *mons veneris*, and Fanny, in this context, seems pretty obvious, not to say blatant. But it may not be quite what it seems. The *Oxford English Dictionary* gives us, as its earliest citation for 'fanny' (in the British slang sense of the word[1]), a quotation from an underground magazine[2] of September 1879: 'You shan't look at my fanny for nothing.' By 1889 the usage was deemed 'common' for 'the female pudenda' by Barrère and Leland's *Dictionary of Slang, Jargon and Cant*. Both of these citations postdate John Cleland's *Fanny Hill* by more than a hundred years. Where was Fanny in the meantime?

Slang, of course, is the most difficult type of language to find in printed sources. Its very nature as a para-language of criminals, tramps, soldiers, teenagers and others with good reasons for maintaining secrecy ensures that it stays out of print. Because of this, the historical origins of many of our common slang words are a subject of endless and often unresolvable debate. Lexicography as a profession long ago threw in the towel over 'fanny'. Eric Partridge, the twentieth century's greatest British slang expert, wrote that its use might even have originated with Cleland: that is, for Cleland, 'Fanny' might merely have been an ordinary first name (short for Frances), and the book could have been entitled *Jane Hill*, or *Mary Hill*, for all the meaning it had. The Partridge line was later taken by slang-hunters such as Jonathon Green and by biographers of Cleland such as William Epstein, who concluded that 'fanny' was 'a possible mid-eighteenth-century slang term for the female pudenda that may or may not have predated the publication of Cleland's book'.

There are some other reasons, aside from simple lexico-graphical despair, for thinking that 'fanny' might indeed have originated with Cleland. Early dictionaries of slang which pull no punches in other areas – such as Frances Grose's *Classical Dictionary of the Vulgar Tongue* of 1785 – do not mention it. And then there is the style of the novel itself. It is a master-piece of evasion. Cleland manages to get through the whole of it without resorting once to obscenity, very likely in an attempt to mollify the censor and avoid prosecution. Cleland knew what it was to spend time in prison: *Fanny Hill* was largely written whilst in the Fleet Gaol for debt, and pub-lished in November 1748 while he was still incarcerated. To have used a slang term for the vagina for the very name of his heroine would have been a dubious way to please. Instead he deployed a whole vocabulary of euphemism and euphuism for the sexual act and the sexual parts. Terms for the female genitals included the 'rose-lipped ouverture', 'sweet seat', 'soft laboratory of love', 'cloven spot', 'embower'd bottom-cavity', 'central furrow', 'treasure of love', 'pleasure-thirsty channel', 'flesh-wound' and 'etcetera'; those for the male parts included the 'weapon of pleasure', 'pleasure pivot', 'love's true arrow', 'plenipotentiary instrument', 'gristle', 'flesh brush', 'animated ivory', 'picklock' and 'whitestaff'. But none of them did him any good. He was released from prison in March 1749 into a storm of protest over his book. The Messengers to the Press, the government body responsible for bringing prosecutions against 'unauthorized and undesirable printing', had decided it was unlawful, and within eight months Cleland was back in custody, this time for obscenity. It took until at least November 1750 to extricate himself from the legal machinery. It was, he reported, very bad for his rheumatism.

But *Fanny Hill* was not originally the title. A notice of the novel's first publication in *The General Advertiser* of November 21, 1748 read:

> *This Day is Published, (Price 3s.)*
> MEMOIRS OF A WOMAN OF PLEASURE.
> Written by a PERSON of QUALITY.
> Printed for G. FENTON, in the Strand.

Fanny made her first appearance in the title in 1750, in a new, one-volume edition entitled *Memoirs of Fanny Hill*, probably edited by Cleland and published to pay off his debts. A century later she had entirely taken over from the 'Woman of Pleasure' format. By 1850 there were at least twenty US and British versions of Cleland's book and numerous others in French, German, Spanish, Portuguese and other languages, the majority of which employed, in the title, the lewd trademark 'Fanny Hill'. There were also scores of imitations, spin-offs and rip-offs, continuing right up to our own times. In the British Library there is *Fanny Hill's Bang-up Reciter, Friskey Songster, and Amarous* [sic] *Toast Master* from 1835; the spurious *Suppressed Scenes from the Memoirs of Fanny Hill* from 1920; *The Daughter of Fanny Hill* from 1967; and *Fanny Hill's Cook Book* from 1972. Whether all this supports or detracts from the case that 'fanny' originated with Cleland is difficult to say. The ascendancy of *Fanny Hill* as a title could be conjectured to coincide with the rise of fanny as a slang term, itself brought into existence by the success of the book; alternatively, the rude intrusion of fanny into the title might reflect the fact that it was a well-known slang term in the first place.[3]

The book exists today in a rather schizophrenic form. For the no-frills paperback reprint market it is *Fanny Hill*. For the 'classics' market, with scholarly introductions and notes, it is *Memoirs of a Woman of Pleasure*. Fanny is both saucy harlot and *demi-mondaine*. We are left to ourselves to decide whether Cleland's novel is an unpretentious slice of porn or a canonical eighteenth-century novel alongside *Tom Jones* and *Humphrey Clinker*.

1 Except perhaps if you are an American, in which case 'fanny' might refer to the backside.

2 The magazine is *The Pearl*, a Victorian 'Journal of Facetiæ and Voluptuous Reading', and the quotation comes from a story perplexingly entitled 'Sub-Umbra, or Sport among the She-Noodles'. The previous month's number of *The Pearl* supplies the quotation for the epigraph to this chapter.

3 Some support for the latter theory is given by *Shamela*, published seven years earlier: see chapter 11. It is dedicated to 'Miss Fanny, &c'. Miss Fanny was Alexander Pope's nickname for John, Lord Hervey, the Lord Privy Seal in the Walpole ministry, and an enemy of the Scriblerus sect (to which Fielding, the author of *Shamela*, allied himself). The significance of this is in the '&c'. The 'etcetera' was an established euphemistic term for the female genitals (Cleland used it, but it was not his own coining). Its pairing with 'Fanny' is suggestive.

13. THE SWISS FAMILY ROBINSON
(1812)

Der Schweizerische Robinson was written by a Swiss pastor, Johann David Wyss. It tells the story of a pious Swiss family, a mother, father and four young sons, marooned on an island in the East Indies following a shipwreck. It is 600 pages long. The father, who narrates the book, uses the shipwreck as a pedagogical opportunity:

> 'I believe,' said Ernest [aged 12], 'that mangoes grow on the sea-shore in marshy soil.'
>
> 'You are partly right, my boy,' I said, 'but what you say applies to the black mango, not to the grey or red species, which bear small berries and do not grow so high.'

The importance of killing things receives heavy emphasis:

> In a few seconds he reappeared carrying an enormous lynx by the hind legs, and turned the animal round for our inspection.
>
> 'Bravo! my young sportsman,' I cried. 'You have rendered a great service to our pigeons and poultry. That fellow would have robbed us of some of them to-night. Take care there is not another in the vicinity. These animals rarely live singly. They must be hunted to death unsparingly if we wish to keep our farm-yard intact.'

During their stay on the island the family undertake a holocaust of its creatures. Among the species butchered are kangaroos, penguins, bears, giant land crabs, capybaras, apes, jackals, ostriches and turtles (the island contains the fauna of six continents). To keep themselves in comfort the family build a luxurious treehouse, plant and harvest corn, milk cows (rescued from the ship), boil up a whale, manufacture isinglass and cochineal, breed doves, gather honey, tap rubber and salt herrings. There is no difficulty of island life that their ingenuity and perseverance cannot resolve. By the end of the book they have created a Calvinist paradise in which nature has been subdued and largely exterminated, and where disease, sex and conflict (between humans) have been banished. In a final act of dour appropriation they christen their island 'New Switzerland'.

The family is not, of course, called Robinson. They are never named. The title refers instead to Defoe's *Robinson Crusoe* of 1719. In an odd twist of literary fate the word 'Robinson' had taken on a life of its own in eighteenth-century European publishing, appearing in the titles of hundreds of adventure stories, mainly German and Dutch, but also French, Danish, Swiss, Swedish and Italian, known collectively as 'Robinsonades':[1] *Teutsche Robinson* (1722), *Americanische Robinson* (1724), *Nordische Robinson* (1741), *Hollandsche Robinson* (1743), *Dänische Robinson* (1750), *Walchersche Robinson* (1752), *Maldivschen Philosophen Robine* (1753), *Oude en Jongen Robinson* (1753), *Isländische Robinson* (1755), *Hartz-Robinson* (1755), *Robinson vom Berge Libonon* (1755), *Haagsche Robinson* (1758), *Robertson* [sic] *aux terres australes* (1766), *Steyerische Robinson* (1791) and *Böhmische Robinson* (1796), among many others, all by different authors. The stories never included anyone called Robinson. 'Robinson' simply denoted an adventure tale. Nor did they necessarily take place on desert islands: there were Robinsonades set on mountain tops, in jungles, among corsairs or in Turkish prisons. Many of the tales dispensed with the idea of the isolated adventurer altogether. There were even Robinsonades without 'Robinson' in the title.

Scholars first began to examine the Robinsonade phenomenon as early as the mid-1700s. Among the Robinsonade subgroups identified by a French scholar were the *robinsonnade gullivérienne*, the *robinsonnade en famille* (such as the *Swiss Family*) and the *robinsonnade de l'enfant*. There were satirical Robinsonades, fantastical Robinsonades, Utopian Robinsonades and interplanetary Robinsonades. Life was a Robinsonade. By the nineteenth and twentieth centuries the Robinsonade had mutated still further: *Tarzan of the Apes*, looked at in a certain way, is a Robinsonade (a *robinsonnade de l'enfant?*), and so is *The Island of Doctor Moreau* and *Lord of the Flies* (dystopian Robinsonades). In film and television, *Lost in Space* was obviously a Robinsonade (being based on the *Swiss Family*), and there were television dramas such as *Mountain Family Robinson* and *Swiss Family Robinson Lost in the Jungle*.

But strangely, of the eighteenth- and nineteenth-century continental Robinsonades, only *The Swiss Family Robinson* took root when transplanted back on to English-speaking soil. Why, it is difficult to say. Perhaps the title had something to do with it. Originally, of course, it had been *Der Schweizerische Robinson*, and as such was indistinguishable from all the other *Hollandsche Robinson*s, *Dänische Robinson*s and *Haagsche Robinson*s. But the insertion of the word 'Family' in translation put it in a class of its own. 'Family' acted as a sort of pivot. Substitute anything for the 'Swiss' or the 'Robinson' and you get an infinite number of delightfully silly variations: *Space Family Robinson, Beverly Hills Family Robinson, Swiss Family Treehouse, Swiss Family Orbison, Swiss Family Guy Robinson, Mouse Family Robinson, Swiss Family Mouse House, Stick Family Robinson, Swiss Bank Family Robinson, Swiss Cheese Family Robinson*, and on and on (all real examples). The words 'Swiss Family Robinson' are close to nonsense in any case: tinkering with them reduces them to gibberish. Perhaps the reason only one Robinson made it back home was because it could be endlessly parodied.

1 The term 'Robinsonade' first appeared in the work of Johann Gottfried Schnabel, and was used to denote an imitation of Defoe's *Robinson Crusoe*.

14. FRANKENSTEIN, OR THE MODERN PROMETHEUS
(1818)

Frankenstein, the book, is rather different from the Universal Studios movie of 1931. In the book there is no forbidding castle. There is no misadventure with the wrong brain. No lightning animates the creature. There is no hunchbacked Fritz. Victor (not Henry) Frankenstein works alone, and he is not a doctor, but a university student. The book is set in the Swiss Alps, London, the Orkney Islands and, most surprisingly of all, the Arctic. There are no lynch mobs of lederhosen-clad villagers. They would be rather cold.

The monster himself, called the 'daemon', has long, flowing hair and is eight feet tall, and no bolts protrude from his neck. His intellectual interests rather surpass those of the Universal Studios monster. Soon after his creation he comes across some discarded copies of Plutarch's *Lives* and some volumes of Milton[1] and Goethe, which he reads hungrily. They awake his finer instincts, but when his creator, Franken-stein, spurns him, he begins to kill, and kill again. He justifies his actions in florid periods indistinguishable from those of both narrator and hero:

> Believe me, Frankenstein, I was benevolent; my soul glowed with love and humanity; but am I not alone, miserably alone? You, my creator, abhor me; what hope can I gather from your fellow creatures, who owe me nothing? They spurn and hate me. The desert mountains and dreary glaciers are my refuge. I have wandered here many days; the caves of ice, which I only do not fear, are a dwelling to me, and the only one which man does not grudge. These

bleak skies I hail, for they are kinder to me than your fellow beings. If the multitude of mankind knew of my existence, they would do as you do, and arm themselves for my destruction. Shall I not then hate them who abhor me?

In the film this becomes one word – 'Uuuuuaaaar-rrnnnnhhhhh!'

The biographical origins of the book – particularly its genesis in a ghost-story writing competition between Shelley and Byron during a 'wet, ungenial summer' on the shores of Lake Geneva in 1816 – are too well known to go over. But the title, *Frankenstein* – a word now inseparable from the monster himself and from the process of blasphemous meddling with nature that brings him into being – is an interesting choice, and may also have had a biographical origin.

In July 1814, two years before the holiday at Lake Geneva, Mary Godwin eloped with Percy Shelley – not for the purposes of marriage, since Percy was already married – to France and then Switzerland, Germany and Holland. She was sixteen and Percy was twenty-one. By all accounts it was a rather miserable trip, made worse by the fact that Mary's stepsister, Jane Clairmont (also called Claire Clairmont), was tagging along.[2] By September 1814 they were all on their way back home, returning by way of the river Rhine through Germany and Holland. As noted in both Mary's and Jane's diaries, on September 2 they moored at Gernsheim in Hesse. From here the threesome would have been able to see, on a hill, a half-ruined castle: the Castle Frankenstein. It was the former home of one Konrad Dippel (1673–1734), also known as Dippel Franckensteina (Dippel of Frankenstein), who in the early eighteenth century had conducted experiments on animal bones and had been expelled from Strasbourg University after an accusation of grave-robbing. Dippel was an alchemist, and had produced an *Arcanum chymicum* (a secret substance, possibly an elixir of life) which he offered to the Landgrave of Hesse in return for being restored to his family estates. As it happened, the Shelley party met three students from the University of Strasbourg around the date of the mooring near Gernsheim, and it is possible that the castle, and its legend, came up as a topic of conversation.

Or is this link altogether too tenuous? A castle, as we have seen, formed no part of Mary Shelley's book. The name of Frankenstein and his reputed experiments are the only points of possible influence, and the name Frankenstein could have arisen from other sources: there is a tale collected by the Brothers Grimm, for example – admittedly published only in 1816, the year that Mary was writing her book, but existing in oral versions previous to that – in which two brothers called Frankenstein slay a dragon. Or Mary could have encountered it elsewhere. The 'Franken' of Frankenstein is a common component of German names such as Frankenthal or Frankenwald, and *stein*, meaning 'stone' is an equally common suffix. The names Frankheim and Falkenstein appear in Matthew ('Monk') Lewis's Gothic horror tales, which she read in 1815, the year before writing *Frankenstein*. Given all this, the idea of the distant castle and its semi-legendary occupant being a likely influence is not a completely convincing one, even if her proximity to the castle that day remains tantalizing.[3]

So perhaps *Frankenstein* was undreamt of until Mary came to write her book by the shores of Lake Geneva in 1816. But one entry from her diary for 1814 does still seem to have a bearing on the book. Apparently the Germans she met on her first trip to the Continent were not very much to her liking. In a rather austere language, she wrote:

> We stopped at Mettingen to dine and there surveyed at our ease the horrid & *slimy* faces of our companions in

voyage – Our only wish was to absolutely anihilate such uncleansable animals, to which we might have adressed the boatmans speech to Pope – Twere easier for god to make entirely new men than attempt to purify such monsters as these.[4]

1 Milton's *Paradise Lost* supplies the epigraph to the book: 'Did I request thee, Maker, from my clay/To mould me man? Did I solicit thee/From darkness to promote me?'

2 'Now I would not go to Paradise with her for a companion – she poisoned my life when young . . . she has still the faculty of making me more uncomfortable than any human being,' Mary wrote later.

3 The subtitle *The Modern Prometheus* is easier to account for. Prometheus was the Titan of Greek myth who stole fire from the gods to benefit humankind. In later Roman versions of the myth, however, particularly in Ovid's *Metamorphoses* – which Mary also read in 1815 – he was more than merely a succourer of humankind, he was a *creator* of human life, or as Ovid termed it, a *plasticator*:

> A creature of a more exalted kind
> Was wanting yet, and then was Man design'd:
> Conscious of thought, of more capacious breast,
> For empire form'd, and fit to rule the rest:
> Whether with particles of heavenly fire,
> The God of Nature did his soul inspire;
> Or earth, but new divided from the sky,
> And, pliant, still retain'd th'ethereal energy:
> Which wise Prometheus temper'd into paste,
> And, mix't with living streams, the godlike image cast [. . .]
> From such rude principles our form began;
> And earth was metamorphosed into man.

Victor Frankenstein is therefore, as a creator of life, the Modern Prometheus of the subtitle.

4 Sunday, August 28, 1814. Original spelling.

15. POEMS BY CURRER, ELLIS AND ACTON BELL
(1846)

One of the most abject failures in the history of publishing occurred in 1846. Three aspiring young authors, Charlotte, Emily and Anne Brontë, using their Aunt Elizabeth's legacy, paid for the publication of a slim volume of their poetry using the pseudonyms Currer, Ellis and Acton Bell. It sold two copies. The hundreds of unsold books that remained – the original edition had been of a thousand – were left languishing in the storerooms of their publishers, Aylott and Jones.

As if anticipating the indifference of the public, the poems presented a world of almost unrelieved gloom. The concentration was on death (particularly young death), illness, betrayal, separation from loved ones by distance or time, the beauty of children and the brevity of childhood, the natural world and its pitilessness, remembrance of the dead, emotional anguish and its forbidden ecstasies, the rapture of death, the tomb, desire for death under the weight of misery, and faith and its fragility. It was a fantastically morbid collection – understandably so, since the Brontës had not only lost their mother at an early age but had witnessed the deaths of two sisters in childhood from tuberculosis, Maria and Elizabeth, in 1825.

The title of the sisters' collection was a gem of cryptography. Each pseudonym was chosen so as to have the same initials as the real sister – CB, EB and AB respectively. Charlotte, writing in 1850 after the deaths of her two surviving sisters (Emily died in 1848 at the age of thirty, and Anne in 1849 at the age of twenty-nine) gave a partial explanation of the names:

Averse to personal publicity, we veiled our own names under those of Currer, Ellis, and Acton Bell; the ambiguous choice being dictated by a sort of conscientious scruple at assuming Christian names positively masculine, while we did not like to declare ourselves women, because – without at that time suspecting that our mode of writing and thinking was not what is called 'feminine' – we had a vague impression that authoresses are liable to be looked on with prejudice; we had noticed how critics sometimes use for their chastisement the weapon of personality, and for their reward, a flattery, which is not true praise.

The sisters thus chose the 'ambiguous' Christian names of Currer, Ellis and Acton (though who would call a girl Acton?) because to take masculine Christian names – say, Christopher, Edward and Andrew Bell – would have been outright deceit, and they feared they would be either sneered at or patronized if they revealed themselves to be female. But why these hermaphroditic names in particular? And why Bell?

Biographers of the sisters agree that Currer was almost certainly for Frances Mary Richardson Currer, one of the founders of the Clergy Daughters School at Cowan Bridge which Charlotte and Emily both attended. Frances Currer was a well-known bibliophile and scholar, and had one of the largest libraries in the north of England. In 1936 the clergyman Thomas Dibdin called her 'the head of all female collectors in Europe' and 'a sort of modern Christina of the North'.

Acton Bell is likely to have come from Eliza Acton, a poetess who had found fame with her first book of poems in 1826. Many of her poems were moodily Brontëan in theme: 'The Grave'; 'On the Death of Ellen Sharp'; 'Let Me Sit in the Twilight Hour Alone'; 'A Shadow, Dark as Death'; 'Go, Cold and Fickle Trifler'; and 'Come to My Grave'. Her most enduring success, however, rested on her cookery book of 1845, the year before the Brontë sisters published their poems. *Modern Cookery for Private Families* went into three editions in the year of its publication, and was still in print by 1914. Elizabeth David called it 'the greatest cookery book in our language'. The fusion, in the person of Eliza Acton, of the wild, the passionate, the morbid and the handily domestic may well have appealed to Anne Brontë.

What then of Ellis Bell? In a 1994 paper the critic Marianne Thormahlen pointed to an intriguing candidate: Sarah Ellis, the author of a number of conduct manuals for girls and women, including *The Daughters of England*, *The Mothers of England*, *The Beautiful in Nature and Art* and *The Education of the Heart*. This is perhaps the most controversial link of the three, given that Sarah Ellis placed much emphasis on woman's worth as a mother and wife; but some of Ellis's other ideas chimed with what we know of the Brontës' views. She argued in *The Mothers of England* that girls should be given the freedom of the outdoors from an early age: 'they should climb the craggy rock, penetrate the forest, and ramble over hill and dale.' Such an idea would have appealed strongly to Emily Brontë. Ellis further urged women to acquire a general knowledge of politics and society, to be conversant with social issues such as slavery, temperance and cruelty to animals, and made frequent and admiring reference to Byron and Scott (the former a Brontë favourite). She reserved special praise for governesses (all the Brontës were trained as governesses):

And here I must beg to call the attention of the mothers of England to one particular class of women, whose rights and whose sufferings ought to occupy, more than they do, the attention of benevolent Christians. I allude to governesses, and I believe that in this class, taken as a whole, is to be found more refinement of mind, and consequently more susceptibility of feeling, than in any other.

And the pseudonymous surname Bell? The traditional explanation is that it derived from the middle name of Patrick Brontë's curate, Arthur Bell Nicholls, who was a novelty in the household in 1845/6, and married Charlotte in 1849. But Bell might also have had a feminine origin. The sisters' immediate concern was to have a name beginning with 'B' to match Brontë, and the 'B' nearest at hand would have been their mother's maiden name, Branwell, shared by their aunt Elizabeth, who had supplied the money for them to publish the poems. The name Branwell itself could not be used, of course, being too immediately recognizable (it was also the name of their errant brother), but removing its middle letters would yield Bell. Might the sisters have chosen Bell as a hidden tribute to their aunt and mother?

The sisters, pleasantly stimulated by their failure, then turned to novel-writing. In 1847, the following year, Charlotte's *Jane Eyre*, Emily's *Wuthering Heights* and Anne's *Agnes Grey* were all accepted for publication, all still under the pseudonyms of Currer Bell, Ellis Bell and Acton Bell. All were immediately successful. The Bell siblings – their sex was still not known, even to their publishers – became famous, and speculation mounted on their true identities. The remaining copies of the 1846 *Poems* were bought up from Aylott and Jones by a new publisher, Smith, Elder & Co., and reissued with new bindings. Sales were brisk. The two copies that had been sold the previous year, with the couple of dozen review and gift copies sent out by Charlotte, were the only ones remaining with the original Aylott and Jones imprint. Fewer than ten are believed to be extant. These copies of the despised little book are now among the most precious rarities of nineteenth-century literature.

16. SONNETS FROM THE PORTUGUESE
(1846)

> Within half an hour of their first meeting, he had shaved
> twice, put on three clean collars, given all his hats to the
> odd-job man, and started reading Portuguese Love
> Sonnets.
>
> P.G. Wodehouse, 'There's Always Golf' (1936)

P.G. Wodehouse was almost certainly remembering
Elizabeth Barrett Browning's *Sonnets from the Portuguese*,
which had an enormous vogue in his Victorian childhood.
'Such purity, sweet humility, lofty self-abnegation, and impas-
sioned tenderness have never before found utterance in verse,'
wrote a reviewer for the *Christian Examiner* in 1862. 'Shakespeare's sonnets, beautiful as they are, cannot be compared
with them, and Petrarch's seem commonplace beside them.'
In 1876 E.C. Stedman declared in his *Victorian Poets* that it
was 'no sacrilege to say that their music is showered from a
higher and purer atmosphere than that of the Swan of Avon.'
This fulsome praise extended to her work in general. The
Eclectic Review of 1862 announced that Elizabeth Barrett
Browning was 'universally now crowned chief woman-poet
of any age or time', one who had 'entered into the scenery, the
mystery, the majesty, the sorrow and the glory of the higher
life'. And yet in the twentieth century her stocks collapsed
quite dramatically. It would now seem foolish to put her anywhere near, say, Emily Dickinson. She is now known almost
exclusively for *Sonnets from the Portuguese*, in particular
Sonnet No. 43: 'How do I love thee? Let me count the ways.'
As for the rest of her large output – works such as *Aurora
Leigh*, *Casa Guidi Windows* and *Poems Before Congress* – it

is hardly read at all, suffering because of its stodgy religiosity and archaic diction ('ween', 'o'er', 'thee', 'thou', 'hast', 'nay', 'fain', 'anear', 'enow', 'wroth', 'doat', 'neath', 'sward', and so on).

Sonnets from the Portuguese has survived as her best-known work chiefly because it is so bound up with the famous story of her love affair with Robert Browning. The two poets met in 1845, and married and fled to the Continent in September 1846, pursued by the incontinent wrath of Elizabeth's father. The *Sonnets* were love poems composed during the affair and shortly before the marriage. They chart a journey almost literally from death to life. Elizabeth was a chronic invalid and feared she might not survive another English winter. Robert revived her:

> Then, love me, Love! look on me – breathe on me!
> As brighter ladies do not count it strange,
> For love, to give up acres and degree,
> I yield the grave for thy sake, and exchange
> My near sweet view of heaven, for earth with thee!

In the *Sonnets* Robert is almost a Christ figure: a kiss from him is 'chrism', he himself is 'God's gift', full of 'divine sufficiencies'.

Elizabeth apparently kept the sonnets secret from Robert until 1849 – three years into the marriage – when she showed them to him at Bagni di Lucca. Robert insisted that she publish them in the forthcoming edition of her *Poems* of 1850, and Elizabeth agreed on the condition that they were disguised as translations. 'Portuguese' was a private joke. Some time before meeting Elizabeth, Robert had read her poem 'From Catarina to Camoens'. It had 'affected him to tears . . . again and again'. In sixteen stanzas, written in a rather inappropriately bouncy rhythm, this poem detailed the last thoughts of the Portuguese maiden Catarina, dying in the absence of her lover, the poet Camoens:

> On the door you will not enter
> I have gazed too long: adieu!
> Hope withdraws her 'peradventure';
> Death is near me, – and not *you*!
> > Come, O lover,
> > Close and cover
> These poor eyes you called, I ween,
> 'Sweetest eyes were ever seen!'

Before he knew anything of the sonnets, Robert's pet name for Elizabeth was his 'Portuguese'. Elizabeth explained in a letter to her sister Arabel in January 1851 that the title 'did not mean (as we understood the double-meaning) "from the Portuguese language" . . . though the public (who are very little versed in Portuguese literature) might take it as they pleased.'

But it might have been very different. At least, according to Edmund Gosse it might. In his 1896 collection *Critical Kit-Kats* he claimed that the title of the book had nearly been (incredibly) *Sonnets from the Bosnian*:

> It was in the second or 1850 edition of the *Poems in two volumes* that the *Sonnets from the Portuguese* were first given to the public. The circumstances attending their composition have never been clearly related. Mr. Browning, however, eight years before his death, made a statement to a friend, with the understanding that at some future date, after his own decease, the story might be more widely told. [. . .]
>
> When it was determined to publish the sonnets [. . .] the question of a title arose. The name which was ultimately chosen, *Sonnets from the Portuguese*, was

invented by Mr. Browning, as an ingenious device to veil the true authorship, and yet to suggest kinship with that beautiful lyric, called *Catarina to Camoens*, in which so similar a passion had been expressed. Long before he ever heard of these poems, Mr. Browning called his wife his 'own little Portuguese,' and so, when she proposed 'Sonnets translated from the Bosnian,' he, catching at the happy thought of 'translated', replied, 'No, not Bosnian – that means nothing – but from the Portuguese! They are Catarina's sonnets!' And so, in half a joke, half a conceit, the famous title was invented.

Without Browning's intervention, then, 'Bosnian' would have been irrevocably associated in English-speaking countries with the muse of love. In this parallel literary universe, the love-struck hero of P.G. Wodehouse's golfing story would have been portrayed giving away his hats, putting on clean collars and reading Bosnian Love Sonnets. Elizabeth Barrett Browning's surviving masterpiece would have had a title rather bolder, rather funnier and rather more outrageously deceitful than the one it finally got. Perhaps Robert should have kept quiet.

17. THE LADY OF THE CAMELLIAS
(1848)

André Maurel reported that on the day of the funeral of Alexandre Dumas *fils* in 1895, mourners took flowers from his grave in Montmartre cemetery and placed them on the nearby tomb of Alphonsine Plessis, the real 'Lady of the Camellias'. Dumas's famous love story, as the entire world knew, was in fact a thinly disguised piece of autobiography. Dumas was the 'Armand Duval' of the book and Alphonsine Plessis was 'Marguerite Gautier'. And now he had gone to join her for ever.

The Lady of the Camellias tells the story of a Parisian courtesan of the era of Louis Philippe. She is a living doll:

> Upon an oval of indescribable loveliness, place two dark eyes beneath brows so cleanly arched that they might have been painted on; veil those eyes with lashes so long that, when lowered, they cast shadows over the pink flush of the cheeks; sketch a delicate, straight, spirited nose and nostrils lightly flared in a passionate aspiration towards sensuality; draw a regular mouth with lips parting gracefully over teeth as white as milk; tint the skin with the bloom of peaches which no hand has touched – and you will have a comprehensive picture of her entrancing face [. . .] Exactly how the torrid life she led could possibly have left on Marguerite's face the virginal, even childlike expression which made it distinctive, is something which we are forced to record as a fact which we cannot comprehend.

When Marguerite enters her box at the theatre, even the eyes of the actors on stage turn to her. She is always seen carrying a bunch of camellias: for five days of the month the fragile blooms are crimson, and on the other twenty-five, white. 'No one ever knew the reason for this variation in colour which I mention but cannot explain.'[1] Her lovers all have asterisks for names. There is the Count de G***, who launches her career as a courtesan, and the Count de N***, who bores her but pays the bills. An elderly duke showers her with diamonds because she reminds him of his dead daughter. But Marguerite has consumption, and fears she has not long to live. The only man she truly loves is Armand Duval, the young and handsome narrator of the novel, who somehow persuades her to relinquish her life of vice and come to the country with him. On a strict goat's-milk diet, her health improves. But Armand's father gets wind of the affair and visits Marguerite secretly: he persuades her to give Armand up for the good name of the family. She agrees, out of love for Armand, and, pretending she has tired of him, returns to her old ways. Armand is fooled and shuns her: Marguerite's health declines and she locks herself in a darkened Paris apartment. Alone, abandoned by all, she dies, spitting blood and screaming Armand's name. After her death Armand learns of her sacrifice and is tortured by remorse and grief. He cannot accept she is dead. He hurries to her grave, which at that moment is being opened so that the body can be transferred to a marble tomb near by. A scene worthy of Poe follows:

'Let's get on with it,' said the superintendent.

At this, one of the men reached out his hand, began unstitching the shroud and seizing it by one end, suddenly uncovered Marguerite's face.

It was terrible to behold, and horrible to relate.

The eyes were simply two holes, the lips had gone, and the white teeth were clenched. The long, dry black hair was stuck over the temples and partly veiled the green hollows of the cheeks, and yet in this face I recognized the pink and white vivacious face which I had seen so often.

It is a bravura counterpart to the 'oval of indescribable loveliness' passage quoted above. Armand, broken but convalescing, confides his story to a friend, and the book ends.

It was well known that the whole thing was a *roman à clef*. Armand Duval was Alexandre Dumas (they even have the same initials), and Marguerite Gautier was Alphonsine Plessis. What was less well known was the true story of Alphonsine's life. Born in Nonant, in Normandy, in 1824, she was the daughter of Marin Plessis, a pedlar, who seems to have sold her for sex to his acquaintances when she was as young as twelve or thirteen. She made her way to Paris, where she became a shop-girl, and where a restaurant owner took a fancy to her. She became his mistress, and as time went by she attracted the attentions of richer and nobler clients. By the age of sixteen she was one of the most sought-after courtesans in Paris, had changed her name to Marie Duplessis, taught herself to read and write, and was celebrated not just for her beauty, but for her wit and elegance. The camellias she favoured were bought from the establishment of M. Raconot in the rue de la Paix. Her protectors now included an elderly Russian diplomat, the Comte de Stackelberg (the model for 'the Duke') and a rich army officer, Comte Édouard de Perregaux (the model for N***). At one time a cabal of seven aristocratic rakes pooled their resources so that one of them could have her each night, and in token of the arrangement presented her with a dressing table containing seven drawers. In 1844 she became the mistress of Alexandre Dumas *fils*, the young and unpublished son of Alexandre Dumas *père* (author of *The Count of Monte Cristo* and *The Three Musketeers*). The relationship lasted around eleven months, but the strains and jealousies of their situation finally brought it to an end. Soon afterwards Marie met the love of her life, the composer Franz Liszt. Liszt, it seems, returned her love, as much as he was able to with pressing sexual duties of his own: 'She was the most absolute incarnation of Woman who has ever existed,' he wrote. But for reasons very probably financial in origin Marie married Perregaux in 1846, at Kensington Registry Office, London. In late 1846 she was very ill. One journalist described her sitting in her box 'the shadow of a woman . . . something white and diaphanous'. Two months later, in February 1847, she was dead, aged twenty-three. Neither Dumas nor Liszt attended her in her final illness.

In June of the same year Alexandre Dumas was in deep trouble. Heavily in debt, he needed a subject for a book. The obvious choice was the life of Marie. He wrote the novel in three weeks that summer, and its success eased his situation a little. But it was when he turned it into a play in 1852 that it became a phenomenon. The first actress to make it a Paris-wide sensation was Eugénie Doche: Sarah Bernhardt carried Marguerite to London and America, and subsequent Marguerites (among them Eleonora Duse and Ida Rubenstein) completed her conquest of the globe. The novel has never been out of print, and has been translated into almost every language. In 1853 Verdi made the story into *La Traviata*, in which Marguerite became Violetta: she has been played by every great diva from Christine Nilsson to Beverly Sills. Scores of films and television dramas have been made of her story, starring everyone from Sybil Thorndike to Greta Scacchi. It has been rewritten from a gay man's point of view, as a graphic novel, as a modern dance piece. Marguerite is a cult. Her tomb in Montmartre remains a site of pilgrimage where fresh camellias are still laid. For some reason, the public is easily, rapturously persuaded that the ultimate price of love is death.

But the plot device on which *The Lady of the Camellias* hinged was a fiction. Marie did not exchange life for death, leaving the vivifying air of the country for Alexandre's sake, to protect his good name. They met, had an affair, quarrelled and parted. The man for whom she seems to have felt the most intense love was Liszt, but there is no Liszt in the novel. Neither is there any mention of Marie's marriage to Perregaux. The Duke, far from being a romantic old man who loved Marie because she reminded him of his daughter, was just another elderly lech, as Dumas later admitted. In the light of all of this, the book takes on a rather different complexion. If you have really loved someone, are you able to cash in on their death a matter of months later, when they are barely cold? *The Lady of the Camellias*, which has survived because it is a beautifully crafted novel of love, is in truth, beneath its glittering surface, a novel of exploitation. One might almost say betrayal.

[1] Dumas knew. The camellias were a sexual traffic-light system. The five 'red' days symbolized her sexual unavailability on those nights, and the white her availability at other times.

18. THE PRELUDE
(1850)

The Prelude was published in the year of Wordsworth's death. It had been kept unpublished at the request of its author since its origins fifty years earlier in 1798.[1] In fourteen books or sections, comprising some 7,900 lines, the poem existed in five different manuscript versions by 1850, none of them with a title. On Wordsworth's death it was given to the printers by his widow, Mary, and published under a title she supplied: *The Prelude*. It was not, however, the prelude to anything, and since Wordsworth was now dead, was never likely to be.

The Prelude is the greatest statement at length of the concerns central to Wordsworth's poetry. The poem immediately pre-dating it is *Lines Composed a Few Miles above Tintern Abbey* (1798), which shares many of the ideas of *The Prelude*, among them the restorative powers of nature, nature's power to shape man's moral being, and the relationship of man and his creations to natural creations:

> These beauteous forms,
> Through a long absence, have not been to me
> As is a landscape to a blind man's eye:
> But oft, in lonely rooms, and 'mid the din
> Of towns and cities, I have owed to them
> In hours of weariness, sensations sweet,
> Felt in the blood, and felt along the heart;
> And passing even into my purer mind,
> With tranquil restoration . . .

That is *Tintern Abbey*. Book I of *The Prelude* reads like a continuation, using the same blank verse:

O there is blessing in this gentle breeze,
A visitant that while it fans my cheek
Doth seem half-conscious of the joy it brings
From the green fields, and from yon azure sky.
Whate'er its mission, the soft breeze can come
To none more grateful than to me; escaped
From the vast city, where I long had pined
A discontented sojourner . . .

The events *The Prelude* describes roughly follow the course of Wordsworth's life. Books I–II deal with his childhood in Cumberland and the animalistic pleasures of playing outdoors in all weathers; Books III–VI detail his education at Cambridge; Book VII deals with London (which he doesn't greatly approve of); Book VIII man and nature; Books IX–XI the French Revolution; and Books XI–XIV the philosophical problems underlying the relationship between the imagination, man and the divine. It was substantially completed by 1805, when it was read by its dedicatee, Samuel Taylor Coleridge, who was sent sections of it while sojourning in Malta (where he was attempting to wean himself off opium). Coleridge pronounced it magnificent. Why, then, was it not published?

The answer is that *The Prelude* was conceived as part of a larger work that Wordsworth and Coleridge had planned together in 1798. This was *The Recluse*, which was to be Wordsworth's *Paradise Lost*. Coleridge wrote many years later of their scheme for *The Recluse*: 'The plan laid out and, I believe, partly suggested by me, was that Wordsworth should assume the station of a man in mental repose, one whose principles were made up, and so prepared to deliver upon authority a system of philosophy. He was to treat man as man, a subject of ear, touch and taste, in contact with external nature, and informing the senses from the mind, and not compounding a mind out of the Senses.' Wordsworth described the same project to a friend as follows: 'I contrive [in it] to convey most of the knowledge of which I am possessed . . . I know not anything that will not come within the scope of my plan.'

It was to consist of three parts. The first, which was begun and abandoned, exists in fragmentary form as the poem *The Ruined Cottage* and a short 'Prospectus'. The second was completed and published in 1814 as *The Excursion*. The third part of *The Recluse* was never begun at all. *The Prelude* (all 7,900 lines of it) was intended merely as the preface to the epic. The conception, then, was truly vast. But *The Recluse* as a whole refused to materialize, despite the fact that Coleridge continually badgered Wordsworth to get on with it.

When publishing *The Excursion*, Wordsworth wrote in the introduction, referring to *The Prelude*:

> The preparatory poem is biographical, and conducts the history of the Author's mind to the point when he was emboldened to hope that his faculties were sufficiently matured for entering upon the arduous labour which he had proposed to himself; and the two works [*The Prelude* and *The Recluse*] have the same kind of relation to each other, if he may so express himself, as the Antechapel has to the body of a Gothic church. Continuing this allusion, he may be permitted to add, that his minor pieces, which have been long before the public, when they shall be properly arranged, will be found by the attentive reader to have such connection with the main work as may give them claim to be likened to the little cells, oratories, and sepulchral recesses, ordinarily included in those edifices.

So the 'minor pieces', by which Wordsworth's reputation is largely secured today (the *Lucy* poems, *Tintern Abbey*,

Ode: Intimations of Immortality, and so on) were merely little 'cells', and *The Prelude* merely an 'Ante-chapel'. The 'Gothic cathedral' of *The Recluse* was to be the work that would bring him imperishable fame. But this work was fated never to exist, and in an important sense, could not exist. *The Recluse* remained a phantom not just because it was unwritten, but because it was unwritable.

The Recluse and *The Prelude* warred with one another in Wordsworth's mind. *The Recluse* was not going to be fun – in fact it was going to be an 'arduous labour', and its subject was going to be life, just that, in general. *The Prelude*, on the other hand, was about one life in particular, Wordsworth's own, a subject which did not require him to do any preliminary reading. *The Recluse* would be huge, vast, formidable; *The Prelude* modest, vernacular, achievable. *The Recluse* was a joint conception entailing a sense of responsibility to Coleridge, *The Prelude* a solo conception, a warm-up exercise allowing Wordsworth to do whatever he liked. *The Recluse* was a duty, *The Prelude* a pleasure. It was an unequal struggle. *The Prelude* began to prey parasitically on the larger work. Soon the tables were turned and *The Prelude* was big, *The Recluse* small. *The Prelude* sucked the life out of *The Recluse*. After writing *The Prelude*, there could never be a *Recluse*, because the last part of *The Prelude* – Books XI–XIV on the imagination, man and the divine – presented the themes that Wordsworth was going to put in *The Recluse*.

Wordsworth tinkered with *The Prelude* throughout his whole career, which is why it exists in five versions. It seems in retrospect a colossal delaying tactic.

Thinking of Wordsworth and Coleridge's youthful designs one thinks of another great Romantic edifice published eight years before *The Prelude*, this time a novel: Nikolai Gogol's *Dead Souls* of 1842. Gogol regarded the first volume of his work merely as 'a pale introduction to the great epic poem which is taking shape in my mind and will finally solve the riddle of my existence', and as 'the front steps of a palace of colossal dimensions' – the last having an unnerving similarity to Wordsworth's 'Ante-chapel . . . to the body of a Gothic church'. In both cases only the portico was ever constructed; the great building went unraised. It was not merely that Gogol or Wordsworth did not have the time, the energy, or, in Gogol's case, the sanity, to finish their work – it was that the work itself was utterly unrealistic to begin with. Both conceptions originated in the intoxication of wishing to include everything, to range across the whole of human experience, to let nothing escape the pen. But both authors are now best loved for their short fictions or short poems, their descriptions of immediate intense moments, the particular and not the general. Wordsworth, who knew so much about the imagination, obviously did not see that if his imagination were allowed complete freedom, paralysis would result. Perhaps a little of Gogol's madness lay behind the fact that *The Prelude* was a prelude to nothing.

1 Wordsworth was exceptionally long-lived as Romantic poets go; he outlived not only Coleridge and Southey, his contemporaries in the first wave of Romanticism, but also Shelley, Keats and Byron.

19. MOBY-DICK
(1851)

Moby-Dick was a real whale. In the days when whales were not sages of the deep but floating oil repositories, sailors were in the habit of giving names to individual whales who were particularly dangerous or unkillable. As Melville wrote in chapter 45 of *Moby-Dick*:

> Was it not so, O Timor Tom! thou famed leviathan, scarred like an iceberg, who so long did'st lurk in the Oriental straits of that name, whose spout was oft seen from the palmy beach of Onibay? Was it not so, O New Zealand Jack! thou terror of all cruisers that crossed their wakes in the vicinity of the Tattoo Land? Was it not so, O Morquan! King of Japan, whose lofty jet they say at times assumed the semblance of a snow-white cross against the sky? Was it not so, O Don Miguel! thou Chilian whale, marked like an old tortoise with mystic hieroglyphics upon the back! In plain prose, here are four whales as well known to the students of Cetacean History as Marius or Sylla to the classic scholar.

One of the most famous, however, and one not mentioned by Melville in the above historical interlude, was 'Mocha Dick', named after the island of Mocha off the Chilean coast. An albino sperm whale (like Moby-Dick), Mocha Dick was said to have drowned over thirty men, sunk five ships and been harpooned nineteen times, which probably accounted for his mood. Melville's chief source was an article by Jeremiah N. Reynolds in the *Knickerbocker Magazine* of 1839 entitled 'Mocha Dick: Or, the White Whale of the Pacific'. He also took from the article the ship's name the *Penguin*, changing it to the *Pequod*. The transformation from Mocha to Moby is rather more difficult to explain, but it may have had its origin in another project that was on Melville's desk at the time he was writing his whale story: this was 'The Story of Toby' about a seafaring friend, Tobias Greene. It may be that 'Toby' influenced the change from Mocha Dick to Moby-Dick.

As well as being the same colour and species as Mocha-Dick, Melville's whale borrowed some of the character of his real-life model. The *Knickerbocker* had described Mocha Dick as possessing a 'lurking deviltry'. In Moby-Dick this became an 'intelligent malignity':

> Nor was it his unwonted magnitude, nor his remarkable hue, nor yet his deformed lower jaw, that so much invested the whale with natural terror, as that unexampled, intelligent malignity which, according to specific accounts, he had over and over again evinced in his assaults. More than all, his treacherous retreats struck more of dismay than perhaps aught else. For, when swimming before his exulting pursuers, with every apparent symptom of alarm, he had several times been known to turn round suddenly, and, bearing down upon them, either stave their boats to splinters, or drive them back in consternation to their ship.
>
> Already several fatalities had attended his chase. But though similar disasters, however little bruited ashore, were by no means unusual in the fishery; yet, in most instances, such seemed the White Whale's infernal afore-thought of ferocity, that every dismembering or death that he caused, was not wholly regarded as having been inflicted by an unintelligent agent.

So much for the title of *Moby-Dick*, one might think. But there is an odd twist in the tale. *Moby-Dick* was not the title of the book at all. The original title was simply *The Whale* – just that – when first published in London by Richard Bentley on October 18, 1851. Now very rare (bound in blue cloth boards and cream cloth spines with a sounding whale gilt-stamped on the spines), the English edition was also substantially different textually from the American Harper edition, which followed one month later on November 14, 1851, and bore the familiar title *Moby-Dick*. The English editor, striving to cram Melville's 'baggy monster' of a book into three volumes, had laid about him with great abandon, hacking out whole chapters and excising anything with any undercurrent or overcurrent of sexual innuendo – which was, and is, a great deal of the book.

The English edition then is a bowdlerized curiosity, and the American edition the definitive, unexpurgated *Moby-Dick*. And as if to give its imprimatur to the true, the pure American edition, an odd circumstance heralded its publication. On November 5, 1851, just nine days before its appearance, news reached New York that the whaler *Ann Alexander*, out of New Bedford, had been rammed and sunk by a whale. Despite stories of vicious and malignant whales, this was still a rare event, and the news spread rapidly throughout the globe. Melville could barely hide his glee. On November 7 he wrote animatedly to his friend Evert Duyckinck:

> Crash! comes Moby Dick himself, & reminds me of what I have been about for part of the last year or two. It is really & truly a surprising coincidence – to say the least. I make no doubt it IS Moby Dick himself, for there is no account of his capture after the sad fate of the *Pequod* about fourteen years ago. – Ye Gods! What a Commentator is this Ann Alexander whale. What he has to say is short & pithy & very much to the point. I wonder if my evil art has raised this monster.

20. THE RING AND THE BOOK
(1868)

In June 1860 Robert Browning was browsing at an open-air flea market in Florence. Among the cheap picture frames and dog-eared prints he came across a battered yellow book. He bought it for one lira – eight pence in English money at the time – and took it home. It proved to be a compendium of legal documents relating to a celebrated murder case of 1698, put together by a lawyer called Francesco Cencini. The picture that emerged from the documents was tragic, squalid and . . . rather entertaining.

In 1693 Count Guido Franceschini, a fifty-year-old nobleman of Arezzo, in somewhat reduced circumstances, decided to take a bride to bolster his fortune. He settled on the thirteen-year-old Pompilia Comparini, a Roman girl with a small dowry. The wedding was speedily arranged in Arezzo, but Pompilia hated her aged, dissolute husband, and after four years of cruelty she decided to run back home to her parents, aided by a young priest who had befriended her, Giuseppe Caponsacchi. The couple were overtaken by Guido at Castelnuovo and arrested on a charge of flight and adultery. It was soon discovered that Pompilia was pregnant – whether by Guido or Caponsacchi it was never discovered – and she was given into the care of an order of nuns for her protection. In December 1697 she was delivered of a baby boy, and went back to live with her parents. Meanwhile Guido was gnashing his teeth, and on January 2, 1698 travelled to Rome with four accomplices and murdered the Comparinis, fatally wounding Pompilia, who died four days later. Guido and his bravoes were arrested, tried and sentenced to death, despite an appeal to the Pope.

Such was the story that Browning gleaned from the various depositions and letters of the yellow book. He realized that he had a subject worthy of an epic poem, but before he could do anything with it, tragedy of his own struck: his wife, Elizabeth, died in June 1861. Browning left Italy for England with his young son, unable to remain at the house, Casa Guidi, where he had enjoyed such a happy married life. The story of the yellow book remained untouched. Browning tried to interest other poets in developing the story, among them Tennyson, but there were no takers. Finally, in 1864, he began himself to work solidly on the poem.

He decided on a poetic structure that mirrored the yellow book. It was to consist of twelve chapters, each reflecting a particular viewpoint as found in the trial material. The monologues included superb portraits of Guido, lecherous and unctuous, and fresh from torture on the rack; Pompilia, dying and sad, telling how she had been sold to a hideous old man who had taken her as she was playing with her toys; Caponsacchi, full of scorn for the legal profession that had failed to protect a child; and the Pope, struggling to come to judgement amid the political and moral complexities of the case. The whole poem was a staggering 21,000 lines long, took Browning four years, and had to be published in four volumes. It was the quintessential High Victorian epic, and made his reputation.

But the yellow book was only half the title. The 'ring' was a gold circlet of Etruscan design, stamped with the letters AEI – Greek for 'evermore' – that had belonged to his wife Elizabeth, and which Browning kept on his watch chain after her death. The poem opens, in a memorable address to the reader, with the ring:

> Do you see this ring?
> 'Tis Rome-work, made to match
> (By Castellani's imitative craft)

Etrurian circlets found, some happy morn,
After a dropping April; found alive
Spark-like 'mid unearthed slope-side fig-tree roots
That roof old tombs at Chiusi . . .

Browning goes on to explain the significance of the ring. It is a symbol of the process of poetic composition. Just as the gold of the ring has been allowed to emerge from the ore surrounding it, so has the story been shaped and rounded from the yellow ore of the yellow book. But a ring is more than a ring. It symbolizes marriage, and the marriage that Browning has in mind is not just the doomed and criminal marriage of the Franceschinis, but his own dead marriage to Elizabeth. Elizabeth seems to breathe everywhere in the poem. As Browning's friend Alexandra Orr put it: 'Its subject had come to him in the last days of his greatest happiness. It had lived with him, though in the background of consciousness, through those of his keenest sorrow. It was his refuge in that aftertime, in which a subsiding grief often leaves a deeper sense of isolation.'

Until *The Ring and the Book*, Browning did not have a wide readership. After its publication in 1868 he was acclaimed as a genius, and earned enough with it to secure himself financially. The *Athenaeum*, which until that point had been hostile to him, declared *The Ring and the Book* to be 'the most precious and profound spiritual treasure that England has produced since the days of Shakespeare'. The reasons for this were to do with the great dramatic achievement of the poem, certainly, but also to do with Elizabeth's death. Elizabeth was celebrated above all for the poetry which expressed her love for Robert (see chapter 16), and now Robert was to be celebrated for his own hymn to Elizabeth. It was the evocation in his title of one of the most famous love stories of the nineteenth century that earned him his final, belated recognition.

21. AROUND THE WORLD
IN EIGHTY DAYS
(1872)

Around the World in Eighty Days, as a title, is simple, descriptive and enticing. As with any title that works superbly well, it has generated a huge number of parodies, puns and spin-offs. A short sample includes: *Around the World in Eighty Ways* (film), *Around the World in Eighty Dreams* (television series), *Around the World in Eighteen Days* (film), *Around the World in Eighty Dates* (book), *Around the World in Ninety Minutes* (documentary), *Around the World in 18 Minutes* (film), *The Three Stooges Go Around the World in a Daze* (film), *Around the World in Eighty Treasures* (television series), *The Simpsons: Around the World in Eighty D'Ohs* (book), and lastly, and inevitably, *Around the World in Eighty Lays* (porn film). And this is only scratching the surface. Of course, it all began with Jules Verne, and his *Le Tour du monde en quatre-vingts jours*. Or did it?

Several theories have been propounded for the origin of *Le Tour du monde*. Verne himself claimed that the idea was sparked in 1871 when he read a newspaper article about a Thomas Cook round-the-world tour package. But there is one man whose career so closely parallels the fictional Phileas Fogg that it would be rash to ignore him: he was an eccentric American railroad magnate called George Francis Train.

Born in 1829, Train began his career as a shipping merchant and opium trader. He made a fortune in gold-dealing in Australia, and was offered the presidency there (which he turned down: he had more important things on his mind). Moving to Britain, he introduced the country's first trams, which were taken up in every major British city and spread throughout Europe. With the fortune he gained from his tramways, he returned to his native land and ploughed all his money into his greatest project, the financing and publicizing of the Union Pacific railroad, the first railroad to connect east and west via the Rocky Mountains. On the way he made another fortune in land deals.

By now Train's ambitions were turning to politics. He began campaigning in 1869 with the ultimate ambition of the US presidency, with the rather unmelodious slogan of 'Get aboard the express train of George Francis Train!' He spoke indefatigably. A journalist of the *Washington Capital* wrote of his oratorical style: 'He double-shuffles and stamps on the floor till the dust obscures him; he beats his breast, clenches his fist, clutches his hair, plays ball with the furniture, outhowls the roaring elements . . . And yet he is not happy; no, he wants to be President.' To another journalist, Train said: 'Of course you know that you are talking to the greatest man in the world. I can give Buddha, Confucius, Moses, Mohammed, and all the rest of them, fifty on the string, and then discount them.'

In the middle of his campaign, 'Citizen Train' announced that he would make a trip around the world in eighty days or less. This might have been a publicity stunt – perhaps he wanted to advertise his new railway and the wonders of super-rapid transportation – but whatever his motives, he started from New York in late July 1870, taking the Union Pacific Railroad to California, and on August 1 shipped on board the *Great Republic* bound for Yokohama. From there he sailed to Hong Kong, then Singapore, the Suez Canal, and Marseilles.

In Marseilles his trip struck the rocks. As he was relaxing in his hotel room, delegates from the Commune burst in upon him and demanded that he speak in favour of the revolution. Train was wealthy and famous, and the revolutionaries needed all the help they could get. 'I told the people that I was in Marseilles on a trip around the world,' Train later wrote, 'but as they had called upon me to take part in their move-ment, I should be glad to repay, in my own behalf, a small portion of the enormous debt of gratitude that my country owed to France for Lafayette.'

Train became embroiled in revolutionary politics. He delivered numerous public harangues and led a march on the military fortifications in Marseilles, which surrendered. In Lyons his luck ran out and he was thrown into prison. After appealing to the international media for help, Train was released, but not before thirteen days of his precious eighty had been wasted. He hot-footed it to Liverpool, where he boarded the steamer *Abyssinia* for New York, and arrived finally in late December, having missed his deadline by at least two months. He claimed he had only taken the stipulated eighty days; no one seemed to be bothered enough to count them, and the papers took up his story. His presidential hopes were soon dashed, however. The 1872 election was won in a landslide by Ulysses S. Grant.

And there the matter might have rested, except for Jules Verne. Verne was already a highly successful writer, having produced several of the *Voyages Extraordinaires* series that included *A Journey to the Centre of the Earth*, *From the Earth to the Moon* and *20,000 Leagues Under the Sea*. But he needed a new idea. In late 1870 and early 1871 news of Train's exploits was arriving in France. Verne, who may have seen the Thomas Cook advertisement but had not yet made the additional conceptual leap from the idea of a leisurely sightseeing trip to a race against time, very probably saw – the coincidences are surely suggestive – the news about Train. He quickly finished the tale of Phileas Fogg and Passepartout and sold the idea as a serial to *Le Temps*, who published it in daily instalments from late 1872. Serialization was a master-stroke. The events seemed to unfold in real time, and were simultane-ously syndicated in newspapers in Britain, the USA and

France. Charles F. Home, who edited Verne's works, wrote: 'Seldom has any piece of fiction excited such a furore. Liberal offers were made to the author by various transportation companies, if he would advertise their routes by having his hero travel by them. And when the final passage of the Atlantic from America to England was to be accomplished, the bids for notice by the various transatlantic lines are said to have reached fabulous sums.'

Verne never acknowledged Train as the inspiration for his book. Train lived on until 1904, and made three more round-the-world trips, beating his record each time, finally achieving sixty days flat. He did not take kindly to Verne's fiction, and once told an English journalist: 'Remember Jules Verne's *Around the World in Eighty Days*? He stole my thunder. I'm Phileas Fogg. But I have beaten Fogg out of sight. What put the notion into my head? Well, I'm possessed of great psychic force.'

22. A STUDY IN SCARLET
(1887)

A *Study in Scarlet*, the book that features the first appearance of Sherlock Holmes, is in some respects rather different from anything that came after it. Watson, recently back from the Afghan Wars with a Jezail bullet in his shoulder, finds Holmes 'conceited', 'querulous', even 'bumptious'. Holmes does not appear to know (or care) that the earth goes round the sun, has never heard of Thomas Carlyle, and professes contempt for any branch of knowledge that will not help him to recover a missing jewel or demonstrate the way out of a locked room. The Holmes of the later stories is a polymath: this Holmes is an anorak. Conan Doyle, at the age of twenty-seven, was finding his way into the character, and, as might be expected, *A Study in Scarlet* shows a great deal of the influence of previous detective fiction, notably the work of Edgar Allan Poe and Emile Gaboriau.

Poe was the most important of all pioneers of detective fiction. His detective, C. Auguste Dupin, appeared in three short works of the 1840s: *The Murders in the Rue Morgue*, *The Mystery of Marie Roget* and *The Purloined Letter*. In Poe we have many of the motifs of the Sherlock Holmes stories: Dupin is a brilliant exponent of the deductive method; a freelance, he lives with the narrator of the stories; he is a master of the testy interruption and the put-down; his method is to eliminate all possibilities, since whatever remains, however improbable, must be the truth. Or as he puts it in *The Murders in the Rue Morgue*:

> Now, brought to this conclusion in so unequivocal a manner as we are, it is not our part, as reasoners, to

reject it on account of apparent impossibilities. It is only left for us to prove that these apparent 'impossibilities' are, in reality, not such.

Conan Doyle's other main influence, Emile Gaboriau, was the creator of the detective Monsieur Vidocq. Vidocq appeared in a number of novels from the 1860s onwards, among them *L'Affaire Lerouge* and *Le Crime d'Orcival*. He was an agent of the Sûreté, regularly consulted a Mycroft-like figure (one Tabaret), and was a connoisseur of footprints and bloodstains. One book in particular, the aforementioned *L'Affaire Lerouge*, had a particular influence on *A Study in Scarlet*. There is a celebrated passage in *A Study in Scarlet* where Watson first sees Holmes at work:

As he spoke, he whipped a tape measure and a large round magnifying glass from his pocket. With these two implements he trotted about the room, sometimes stopping, occasionally kneeling, and once lying flat on his face. So engrossed was he that he appeared to have forgotten our presence for he chattered away to himself under his breath the whole time, keeping up a running fire of exclamations, groans, whistles, and little cries suggestive of encouragement and hope. As I watched him I was irresistibly reminded of a pure-blooded, well-trained foxhound as it dashes backwards and forwards through the covert, whining in its eagerness, until it comes across the lost scent.

Here is Gaboriau's Lecoq in *L'Affaire Lerouge*:

. . . he darted into the inner chamber. He remained there about half an hour; then came out running, then re-entered and then came out again; once more he disappeared and re-appeared again almost immediately. The magistrate could not help comparing him to a pointer on the scent, his turned-up nose even moved about as if to discover some subtle odour left by the assassin. All the while he talked loudly and with much gesticulation, apostrophising himself, scolding himself, uttering little cries of triumph or self-encouragement . . . the investigating magistrate began to grow [im-] patient, and asked what had become of the amateur detective. 'He is on the road,' replied the corporal, 'lying flat in the mud.'

This is very close. The first paragraph, with its central metaphor of the hound on the scent, its little cries and exclamations, its fevered activity and its lying flat on the ground, is almost a paraphrase of the second.

Gaboriau and Poe, then, were clear influences. They were both writers of international reputation, and Conan Doyle read them and knew them. They were not writers from whom he furtively cribbed: they were the Titans of the field, whose mastery it was pointless to gainsay. Doyle made his debt explicit – in a rather sly way – in the second chapter of *A Study in Scarlet*:

'It is simple enough as you explain it,' I said, smiling. 'You remind me of Edgar Allen Poe's Dupin. I had no idea that such individuals did exist outside of stories.'

Sherlock Holmes rose and lit his pipe. 'No doubt you think that you are complimenting me in comparing me to Dupin,' he observed. 'Now, in my opinion, Dupin was a very inferior fellow. That trick of his of breaking in on his friends' thoughts with an apropos remark after a quarter of an hour's silence is really very showy and superficial. He had some analytical genius, no doubt; but he was by no means such a phenomenon as Poe appeared to imagine.'

'Have you read Gaboriau's works?' I asked. 'Does Lecoq come up to your idea of a detective?'

Sherlock Holmes sniffed sardonically. 'Lecoq was a miserable bungler,' he said, in an angry voice; 'he had only one thing to recommend him, and that was his energy. That book made me positively ill. The question was how to identify an unknown prisoner. I could have done it in twenty-four hours. Lecoq took six months or so. It might be made a text-book for detectives to teach them what to avoid.'

This, of course, is irony: Conan Doyle is playing up the 'conceited', 'querulous' Holmes that would later modulate into the omniscient, Olympian Holmes. Holmes is exhibiting imperfect self-knowledge: breaking in on his friends' thoughts is a quintessential Holmesian tactic.

It was an irony rather lost on some of Conan Doyle's contemporaries. There were frequent accusations that he had stolen from Poe and Gaboriau. One of the most stinging attacks was by Arthur Guitermann in his poem of 1915, 'The Case of the Inferior Sleuth':

Holmes is your hero of drama and serial;
All of us know where you dug the material
Whence he was moulded – 'tis almost a platitude;
Yet your detective, in shameless ingratitude –
Sherlock your sleuthhound with motives ulterior
Sneers at Poe's Dupin as 'very inferior!'
Labels Gaboriau's clever 'Lecoq', indeed,
Merely 'a bungler', a creature to mock, indeed!
This, when your plots and your methods in story owe
More than a trifle to Poe and Gaboriau,

Sets all the Muses of Helicon sorrowing.
Borrow, Sir Knight, but be decent in borrowing!

Conan Doyle made reply[1] with a matching twelve-line stanza in dactylic tetrameters:

Have you not learned, my esteemed commentator,
That the created is not the creator?
As the creator I've praised to satiety
Poe's Monsieur Dupin, his skill and variety,
And have admitted that in my detective work
I owe to my model a deal of selective work.
But is it not on the verge of insanity
To put down to me my creation's crude vanity?
He, the created, would scoff and would sneer,
Where I, the creator, would bow and revere.
So please grip this fact with your cerebral tentacle:
The doll and its maker are never identical.

This perhaps seals the matter. Except for one last thing: the title. If Conan Doyle had meant merely to steal from Gaboriau and not acknowledge the fact, would he have called his book *A Study in Scarlet*? For *A Study in Scarlet* is an English-French pun. It echoes the very book that seems to have influenced him most: *L'Affaire Lerouge*.

1 'To an Undiscerning Critic', in Haining, Peter: *The Final Adventures of Sherlock Holmes* (1981)

23. THE KREUTZER SONATA
(1889)

Beethoven completed his Sonata No. 9 for violin and piano, known as the Kreutzer Sonata, in 1802. It consists of three movements, the first a passionate presto (strictly speaking, a presto within an adagio), the second a placid andante, and the third another presto. Its dedicatee was the violinist Rodolphe Kreutzer.

Tolstoy was a great admirer of Beethoven and was himself a talented pianist. On July 3, 1887 he was present at a private performance of the Kreutzer Sonata by his son Sergey at the piano, with Sergey's music teacher on the violin. During the first movement, Tolstoy was seen to rise from his chair and go to the window, where he gave a sob of emotion.

In the spring of the following year another concert was given of the same work, with the same performers. Present on this occasion were the painter Ilya Repin and the actor V.N. Andreyev-Burlak. After the performance Tolstoy made a proposal to the actor and the painter: he, Tolstoy, would produce a story inspired by the Kreutzer Sonata, Repin would paint a canvas based on the story, and Andreyev-Burlak would recite the work at a gathering where the painting would be displayed behind him. As it happened, Andreyev-Burlak died shortly afterwards and Repin never painted the canvas. Tolstoy did write the story, however, and it was published as part of his *Complete Works* in 1891.

This, then, is the ostensible origin of the novel (or novelette) *The Kreutzer Sonata*. Its thematic origin however was in the marriage of Tolstoy and his wife Sofya. The title was, in a sense, tacked on to a theme which had been preoccupying him for years: wedded lust.

Leo Tolstoy had married Sofya Andreyevna Bers in 1862. She was eighteen and he thirty-five, and at first the pair were very happy. With Sofya's untiring clerical support, Tolstoy spent the 1860s and 1870s writing *War and Peace* and *Anna Karenina*. It was during this blissful period that Tolstoy also produced a fragment of a tale called *The Wife-Murderer*.

Then in the late 1870s the marriage began to crumble. More and more children had arrived, some unwanted. By the 1880s Leo and Sofya were quarrelling bitterly. Sex, quarrelling, making up and producing more children (Sofya had over a dozen confinements) was a never-ending cycle. Their diaries and letters show that both husband and wife, in their different ways, felt tormented by their own sexual being. Tolstoy had by now given up (or was struggling to give up) red meat, tobacco, alcohol and comfortable clothes: these things were linked in his mind with sensual and sexual excess. He was also making drafts of a story 'on the theme of sexual love', which may have been a continuation of his earlier story of sexual jealousy, *The Wife-Murderer*. The theme of man's sexual nature and its place in a Christian marriage was preying on his mind.

It was in this atmosphere that Tolstoy heard the two performances of the Kreutzer Sonata in 1887/8. After the second performance in 1888, an act of mental fusion took place, and the three things – the unfinished fictions on sexual love, his own personal sexual predicament, and Beethoven – combined to create *The Kreutzer Sonata*.

In the story, the narrator, Pozdnyshev, discovers – or thinks he has discovered – that his wife is having an affair with a musician, a virtuoso violinist, and murders her in a fit of rage. The plot is skeletal. The story is, in fact, a pretext for a series of highly entertaining diatribes, in the voice of Pozdnyshev, about sex, marriage, prostitution (which is identified with marriage as its unlicensed form), the relations of men and women, and our true destiny as children of God.

Tolstoy's letters and diaries of the period reveal that the true voice of *The Kreutzer Sonata* is not Pozdnyshev's but Tolstoy's. Here is Tolstoy, writing to his son Ilya in 1888, shortly before Ilya's marriage:

> The goal of our life should not be to find joy in marriage, but to bring more love and truth into the world. We marry to assist each other in this task. The most selfish and hateful life of all is that of two beings who unite to enjoy life.[1] The highest calling is that of the man who has dedicated his life to serving God and to doing good . . .

Here is Pozdnyshev:

> For as long as mankind endures, it will follow some ideal – not, needless to say, the ideal of pigs and rabbits, which is to reproduce themselves as abundantly as possible [. . .] but the ideal of goodness, goodness that is attained by means of abstinence and purity.

Here is a letter from Tolstoy to his disciple Chertkov in 1888:

> Sexual intercourse when the woman is not ready to conceive (i.e. when she has no menstrual periods) is without rational justification, and is merely a form of carnal pleasure – and a very ignominious and shameful pleasure, as every man of conscience will admit, being similar to the most infamous, unnatural sexual perversions.

Here is Pozdnyshev:

> You'll notice that the animals copulate with one another only when it's possible for them to produce offspring;

but the filthy king of nature will do it any time, just so long as it gives him pleasure. More than that: he elevates this monkey pastime into the pearl of creation, into love.

Sex, then, for Tolstoy, was base and shameful, and during pregnancy – for this is what he means by 'when she has no menstrual periods' – is an 'infamous perversion'. But his wife was pregnant a good deal of the time, and, as his diaries show, he and Sofya were regularly having sex, pregnant or not. Women in general he found well-nigh irresistible. He poured all of his desire and disgust into *The Kreutzer Sonata*, and it became, not surprisingly, the most sensational of his works to date. When it was first published in manuscript form in 1889 (it was released without Tolstoy's permission and then copied and recopied by the thousand), friends would greet one another in the street not with 'How are you?' but with 'Have you read *The Kreutzer Sonata*?'

Central to the book is the idea of music as the most sensual of the arts. 'Take that *Kreutzer Sonata*, for example,' says Pozdnyshev. 'Take its first movement, that presto: can one really allow it to be played in a room with women in low-cut dresses?' It was the presto that had caused Tolstoy to rise from his chair and begin to sob.[2] Referring to the violinist who steals his wife, Pozdnyshev says:

> This man, because of his outward elegance, his novelty and undoubted musical talent, would, as a result of the intimacy arising out of their playing together, and of the effect produced on impressionable natures by music, especially violin music, inevitably not only appeal to her, but would unquestionably and without the slightest hesitation conquer her, crush her, twist her round his little finger, do with her anything he wanted . . .

Sofya, whose relations with her husband had now deteriorated to the point where she was thinking of running away or finding another man, felt repudiated and humiliated by *The Kreutzer Sonata*. It made a mockery of her years of devotion as a wife and mother, and seemed to represent her as the main hindrance to her husband's spiritual growth. The amount of autobiographical detail in *The Kreutzer Sonata* is remarkable. An especially telling detail is that Pozdnyshev gives his wife his diary to read before their marriage, and as a result shocks her greatly: exactly the same thing had happened, with the same result, between the Tolstoys. Sofya knew that everybody, all her friends, would recognize these autobiographical elements. And she even had to copy it all out.

The Kreutzer Sonata represents a crisis in Tolstoy's spiritual life that led him away from the great mid-period works – *War and Peace* and *Anna Karenina* – and into the late works of Christian anarchism such as *The Kingdom of God is Within You*. It was a transition not without pain. When Tolstoy heard that passionate presto and burst into sobs, what was going through his mind? Was he thinking of the beauty of the world of sensual pleasure, and of its evil, and of the impossibility of goodness? Was he saying goodbye in his heart to those things he would have to renounce in the name of Jesus Christ?

1 It would be interesting to see these sentences incorporated into a Tolstoyan marriage service. For the complete antithesis of this position, see chapter 36 on *The Escaped Cock*.

2 The first presto was, for Tolstoy, the most interesting of the three movements. Amid its rapid see-sawing arpeggios and descending ladders of scales are long notes that can sound like shrieks or groans.

24. THE PICTURE OF DORIAN GRAY
(1890)

At the beginning of 1892, stories were appearing in the London press claiming that Dorian Gray, the hero of Wilde's notorious book, was modelled on a real person, a minor poet named John Gray. They said that John Gray was a protégé of Wilde's, a person under his 'protection'. Wilde acted to scotch the rumours. In late February 1892 he wrote in a letter to *The Daily Telegraph*:

> Allow me to state that my acquaintance with Mr John Gray is, I regret to say, extremely recent, and that I sought it because he had already a perfected mode of expression both in prose and verse. All artists in this vulgar age need protection certainly. Perhaps they have always needed it. But the nineteenth-century artist finds it not in Prince, or Pope, or patron, but in high indifference of temper, in the pleasure of the creation of beautiful things, and the long contemplation of them in disdain of what in life is common and ignoble, and in such felicitous sense of humour as enables one to see how vain and foolish is all popular opinion, and popular judgment, upon the wonderful things of art. These qualities Mr John Gray possesses in a marked degree. He needs no other protection, nor, indeed, would he accept it.
>
> I remain, sir, your obedient servant,
> Oscar Wilde.

Wilde had published *The Picture of Dorian Gray* in *Lippincott's Magazine* in June 1890, and therefore, since his acquaintance with John Gray had been 'extremely recent',

John Gray could not have anything to do with 'Dorian' Gray. This though was false.

John Gray was born into a poor family in Islington in 1866. At a young age he began work in a forge at the Woolwich Arsenal, later becoming a boy clerk in the offices there. In 1882 he took a civil service examination and qualified as a clerk at the Post Office Savings Bank. In 1887 he rose still further by passing the matriculation examination for London University, maintaining himself by continuing in his work as a clerk. He then transferred to the postal department of the Foreign Office. This was a remarkable vaulting of class barriers by the standards of the time, and around 1887 he vaulted still higher by making the acquaintance of some of the figures in the circle of Wilde: Charles Ricketts, Charles Shannon, Ernest Dowson, Arthur Symons and others. John's good looks, it seems, were much appreciated. Early photographs show a young man of some beauty: a very white, smooth skin; a strong, rounded nose and chin; delicate, well-formed lips; and short, dark curling hair.

Gray and Wilde began to be seen together increasingly at parties, dinners, the theatre, galleries, the opera, and at the Café Royal. Gray was now writing his own poetry, much of it in the 'decadent' style of the 1890s. In the poem 'Complaint', dedicated to the French aesthete and anarchist Félix Fénéon, first appearing in Gray's collection *Silverpoints* in 1893 but probably composed a couple of years earlier, he wrote:

> Men, women call thee so or so;
>> I do not know.
>> Thou hast no name
> For me, but in my heart a flame
>
> Burns tireless, neath a silver vine.
>> And round entwine

Its purple girth
All things of fragrance and of worth.

Thou shout! Thou burst of light! Thou throb
Of pain! Thou sob!
Thou like a bar
Of some sonata, heard from far

Through blue-hue'd veils! When in these wise,
To my soul's eyes,
Thy shape appears,
My aching hands are full of tears.

Here are many of the recurring motifs of decadent poetry: the homoerotic ardour; the overblown colour-vocabulary; the botanical metaphors.[1]

There is no doubt that by 1890 Wilde was referring to John as 'Dorian'. Several lines of evidence support this. Ernest Dowson wrote in a letter of November 1890 (after the publication of *The Picture of Dorian Gray* in its magazine form in June that year, but before the appearance of the book in April 1891): 'Thursday at Horne's was very entertaining: [. . .] "Dorian" Gray [read] some very beautiful and obscure versicles in the latest manner of French Symbolism.' The writer Lionel Johnson, shortly after meeting John in the early 1890s, wrote: 'I have made great friends with the original of Dorian: one John Gray, a youth in the Temple, aged thirty, with the face of fifteen.'[2] Arthur Symons recalled that he had been introduced by Wilde to 'the future Dorian Gray' at some point around the end of 1890. And John Gray himself signed one surviving letter to Oscar, of January 1891, 'Yours ever, Dorian'. So when Wilde wrote in *The Daily Telegraph* in 1892 that his friendship with John Gray was of 'extremely recent' origin, this was not the truth. He had known him for several years. It is likely that the lie was an attempt by Wilde to protect Gray, in his position at the Foreign Office, from the scandal that was already attaching to Wilde and would eventually break over his head in March 1895.

Why 'Dorian' though? Almost certainly it was a reference to the 'Greek love'[3] – a phrase which appears frequently in the literature of the period – of Plato's *Symposium* and other works.

In the 1890s there were a number of competing words for homosexuality. The word 'homosexual' had been invented, along with 'heterosexual', by the Hungarian-German writer Károly Mária Kertbeny in around 1868, but had failed to catch on. Instead there were other terms – 'Uranian' was common for male homosexuals, in reference to the god Uranus, who had given birth to Aphrodite without intervention from any woman (Aphrodite had stepped from the foam produced when his testicles were cut off and thrown into the sea). Others favoured 'unisexual' (for example the writer Marc André Raffalovich, a lifelong close friend of Gray, who wrote a treatise on homosexuality) or 'invert' ('inversion' was a neutral term with no pejorative connotations, used by the sexologist Havelock Ellis, among others). 'Dorian' was merely one more way, perhaps more coded than others, to signify 'homosexual'.

Whether Wilde and Gray were ever lovers is not known. The friendship however did not long survive the publication of *The Picture of Dorian Gray*. Gray was displaced by Alfred Douglas (to whom he bore a physical similarity) in 1892, and Gray broke with Wilde completely in 1893.

Gray went on to publish numerous other collections of poetry, critical works and other books, but his later life – almost his whole life, considering how young he was when he mixed with the Wilde circle – was in notable contrast to his 'decadent' youth. He resigned his position at the Foreign

Office in 1897 and in 1898 enrolled at the Scots College seminary in Rome, where he trained for the Roman Catholic priesthood. From 1901 until his death in 1934 he was not Dorian Gray, nor John Gray, but 'Father Gray'.

1 The decadent style was parodied by Owen Seaman in his poem 'Disenchantment':

> My love has sickened unto Loath,
> And foul seems all that fair I fancied –
> The lily's sheen a leprous growth,
> The very buttercups are rancid.

2 In fact John was around twenty-five.
3 The Dorian Greeks were a tribe that descended into the Greek peninsula around 1000 BC.

25. THE SEAGULL
(1895)

In 1892 Anton Chekhov was a success. He had two plays
behind him (*Ivanov* and *The Bear*), and had published many
of the short stories that, to Russian readers, constitute his
greatest work. He was wealthy enough to buy a country
estate for his family in the village of Melikhovo, about fifty
miles from Moscow, and here he began to settle into the role
of a country landowner – a role later mined for stories such as
'New Villa' and 'My Wife'. The house at Melikhovo was
always full of guests: poets, painters, actors and actresses,
doctors, holidaymakers, distant relatives, all sleeping here,
there and everywhere, sometimes spilling out on to mattresses
in the halls. He became a local benefactor and unpaid general
physician to the peasantry (he was, of course, a doctor by
training). He also took to shooting wild game for sport, *à la*
Turgenev.

In the spring of 1892, Chekhov and a friend, Isaac
Levitan, set out from Melikhovo for a day's hunting. Neither
was very experienced with guns. Levitan was actually a landscape painter, more interested in observing the scenery than
shooting bits of it, and both were to some degree aware that
they were play-acting. At one point Levitan, taking aim,
downed a woodcock, and they both ran to find it. When they
discovered its body in the grass they were disconcerted to find
that it was still alive and staring up at them in mute agony.
Levitan pleaded with Chekhov to finish it off. Chekhov
refused, sickening of the whole business. Levitan persisted.
Finally Chekhov, in disgust, smashed the woodcock's head in
with his rifle butt. 'And while two idiots went home and sat
down to dinner,' Chekhov wrote to his friend Alexei Suvorin

on April 8, 1892, 'there was one beautiful, infatuated creature less in the world.'

Three years later Chekhov was writing the first of his major dramatic works. On October 21, 1895, he wrote to Suvorin from Melikhovo: 'I am writing a play which I probably will not finish until the end of November. I am writing it with considerable pleasure, though I sin frightfully against the conventions of the stage. It is a comedy with three female parts, six male, four acts, a landscape (view of a lake), lots of talk on literature, little action and tons of love.' It was *The Seagull*, and the incident with Levitan became its central metaphor.

In *The Seagull*, a loose colony of artists and malcontents – rather similar to the ménage at Melikhovo – live in a house by the shore of a lake, and seek ways to escape the boredom of their existence. An actress, Irina Arkadina, fears age; her son Kostya, a budding writer, is in love with Nina, a pretty neighbour; Nina loves Trigorin, a Hamlet-like writer who is obsessed with his sense of failure as an artist; and Arkadina's brother Sorin completes the main cast with numerous moody speeches about his own inadequacy. At one point Kostya shoots a seagull and brings it into the house. Nina and Trigorin later notice it discarded on a table:

TRIGORIN: What's this?

NINA: A seagull. Kostya killed it.

TRIGORIN: A fine bird. I don't really want to leave here. Try to persuade Irina Arkadina to stay, eh? *(Makes a note in his book.)*

NINA: What are you writing?

TRIGORIN: Just a note or two. Had an idea for a story. *(Puts the book away.)* An idea for a short story: a young girl like you has been living all her life by a lake. She loves it like a seagull and is as free and happy as a seagull.

Then a man happens to come along, sees her and destroys her just for the fun of it, like this seagull.

By the end of the play Nina has become pregnant by Trigorin but has lost her baby. Trigorin has deserted her. Kostya has committed suicide with the gun he used to kill the seagull. Everyone else has sunk further into the slough of despond. Trigorin has had the seagull stuffed for no reason that anyone can remember, and it remains on stage as a piece of heavy symbolism of the type Chekhov didn't often indulge in; it has come to represent Nina's fate at the hands of Trigorin, who has previously, of course, been heartless enough to predict it to her face. Nina says on the last page: 'I'm the seagull.'

It seems highly likely that Chekhov's use of the wild bird – given a species-change for Coleridgean resonance – and his disgust for anyone who destroys a life 'just for the fun of it' were linked to the woodcock incident.

Isaac Levitan, who had thus proved instrumental in the creation of a Chekhov motif, also cropped up oddly in another work, also inspired by events in that first year at Melikhovo.

In the short story *The Grasshopper* (1892), Ryabovsky, a spoilt, handsome landscape artist, has an affair with Olga, the wife of Dymov, a young doctor. Ryabovsky soon tires of Olga and tries to get rid of her, but meanwhile Dymov has become so miserable because of his wife's infidelity that he commits suicide – by sucking the diphtheria poison from a young boy's neck through a pipette, in an attempt to save his life.

Levitan was convinced that Ryabovsky was modelled on him, and on his affair with Sofia Kuvshinnikova, a doctor's wife and friend of Chekhov. The parallels were certainly there – Levitan was also, of course, a landscape painter, and had a reputation as a ladies' man. The character of Dymov, in this scheme of things, could represent Chekhov himself: a young doctor who works hard and provides for all the artistic wastrels around him. ('If I were a landscape painter,' Chekhov later wrote, 'I'd lead an all but ascetic life: I'd have intercourse once a year and food once a day.') After the story was published, Levitan refused to speak to Chekhov, and Sofia Kuvshinnikova refused Chekhov entry into her house. Chekhov denied all charges. A rapprochement with Levitan was effected only two and a half years later.

The Seagull, meanwhile, fruit of that traumatic hunting experience with Levitan, was one of the worst-received plays in the history of the stage. On the opening night on October 17, 1896, when Nina began to give her famous (and slightly ludicrous) speech beginning 'Men, lions, eagles and quail, antlered deer, geese, spiders, silent denizens of the deep . . .' the audience began laughing, booing and catcalling, and didn't stop until the final curtain. Chekhov stormed from the theatre in angry humiliation, vowing: 'If I live seven hundred years, I'll never give the theatre another play.' What began with the death of a bird nearly ended with the death of a career. Three years were to elapse before Chekhov felt able to try another 'sin against the conventions of the stage': *Uncle Vanya*.

26. UBU ROI
(1896)

Père Ubu – Papa Ubu, or just plain Ubu – is one of the most alluringly disgusting characters in the history of theatre. Enormously fat and ugly, wearing a strange costume with a spiral painted on his paunch, continually shouting orders, he is a living marionette, a sort of cross between Mr Punch and the Emperor Bokassa. As *Ubu Roi* opens we witness him plotting to depose the King of Poland. Beside him are his henchmen and his wife, the slatternly Mère Ubu. Also at his right hand is a torturing engine called the *machine à decerveler*, or 'de-braining machine' ('See the brains spurt out!' 'Soon my wife and I are going to be white with splattered brains!'). His speech is a torrent of schoolboy obscenity, literary-philosophico-scientific nonsense, oaths ('by my green candle!') and baby talk, much of it all but incomprehensible, even in French. The first word of the play is '*Merdre!*' Not *merde*, but *merdre*, with an extra 'r', the addition of which seems designed to heighten its obscenity. Among Ubu's tricks is to throw a soiled toilet brush into the pot of food from which his soldiers are eating.

At the first performance of *Ubu Roi* at the Théâtre de l'Oeuvre on December 10, 1896 there was pandemonium. Parisian theatre-goers of the 1890s had become used to a comfortable diet of farce and melodrama, and after the first, long-drawn-out bawl of '*Merdre!*' the audience rose in outrage. Amid the jeering, stamping and shouting, the actor playing Ubu tried to establish order by blowing into a horn, and it was at least fifteen minutes before the play could continue. The press reaction was universally hostile. *Ubu Roi* appeared to reject everything: any recognizable conception of theatre, any notion of satire, even a conventional idea of the unconventional – its bawdy, for example, was not the knowing innuendo of adults but the silly jokes of schoolboy virgins. It was in places deliberately lame and unfunny. It must have been utterly baffling. Reviewers condemned it for its pointless vulgarity, lack of wit, irresponsibility and artistic vacuousness. One reviewer appeared to wish to delouse himself after the performance, writing: 'Despite the late hour, I have just taken a shower. An absolutely essential preventative measure when one has been subjected to such a spectacle.' It all seemed to have been conceived by a naughty child to hoax the grown-ups. And in a sense, it was.

The phenomenon of Ubu began as a schoolboy burlesque, the creation of Alfred Jarry and his friends at the Lycée de Rennes in the late 1880s. The prototype for Ubu was his school physics master, M. Hébert. This unfortunate peda-gogue, incompetent, fat, unable to keep order, was routinely mocked by the children as Père Heb, Éb, Ébouille, Ébé, P.H. and so on. His tormentors, year after year, had constructed a mythology around him: he had been born on the banks of the Oxus River, the son of a Tartar witch and a member of a race known as the *Hommes-Zénormes*, emerging from the womb complete with bowler hat, check trousers and three teeth, one of stone, one of wood and one of iron. He had travelled to the Bering Straits, where he had become trapped in a glacier for a thousand years, but after his release had made his way to France, where he had taken a baccalauréat and become a brigand (naturally), dealing with his enemies by the use of a 'de-braining spoon'. Jarry became the lead archivist of this oral tradition, and M. Hébert's lead tormentor. A school-friend, Henri Hertz, wrote:

He entered the fray at the end, like a matador in a bull-ring, for the death-blow. Complete silence. Coldly, inci-sively, he put to Père Heb insidious, preposterous questions, which caused him to falter in mid-sentence and shattered his composure. He encircled him and made him giddy with his sophistry. He wore him out. Père Heb became disconcerted, batted his eyelids, stammered, pretended not to hear, lost ground. Finally, giving way, he collapsed on to the table . . .The class looked upon the victor Jarry with wonder.

With fear and a sense of recoil also. For there was the distinct feeling that his sarcasm went beyond the general unruliness, that something deep down inside him was taking part in this battle, something different, that his tactics arose from some powerful impulse.

'Père Heb' began to star in various marionette plays that Jarry performed with his friends. At some point in the early 1890s the name Ubu emerged from Ébé and Ébouille. By now his earlier collaborators were beginning to slip away into jobs or the army, and Jarry went to Paris, where he continued writing and polishing the Ubu saga, which was eventually to comprise a cycle of plays beginning with *Ubu Roi* and including *Ubu Cocu* and *Ubu Enchainé*. In the Symbolist Paris of the 1890s he found a place where eccentrics of all kinds were tolerated. Numerous tales were told about him. He would enter a restaurant and demand to be served the last course first, proceeding via the main course to the *hors d'oeuvre*. He was once asked for a light by a stranger in the street and discharged a pistol shot (*un feu*). When some children were endangered by his pistol practice, he told their mother: 'Please do not worry, Madame, if any unfortunate event should occur, we will soon engender others by you.' André Gide wrote of his 'bizarre, relentless manner of speaking, without inflexion or nuance, with an equal emphasis on every syllable, including the mute "e"s. Had a nutcracker spoken, it would have done so in exactly the same way.' After the success of

Ubu Roi in 1896 he became famous overnight, and began to adopt the language and demeanour of his creation.

For a long time after his death in 1907 (aged thirty-four) Jarry was given only a token place in the history of the theatre. After the Second World War however, a strange organization was formed, the 'Collège de 'Pataphysique', whose members included Jacques Prévert, Max Ernst, Eugène Ionesco, Marcel Duchamp, Francis Picabia and René Clair. 'Pataphysics (the initial apostrophe is deliberate and silent) had been Jarry's attempt to synthesize his philosophy: in its briefest formulation it is 'the science of imaginary solutions'. The Collège championed all of Jarry's works (which included many further novels and plays), and the 1950s and 1960s saw the export of the Ubu plays to the USA, Britain and elsewhere. The Jarry phenomenon, fifty years late, was beginning to roll. It became clear that his work stood as an important precursor to movements such as Dada, Surrealism and the Theatre of the Absurd. A certain strain of childish vulgarity, anti-sense and anti-wit in modernism could in fact be attributed directly to Jarry. Père Ubu, born of a malicious desire to destroy a hated teacher, was now venerated as the totem of those who wished to dismantle the world of grown-up rationality.

27. THE PLAYBOY OF
THE WESTERN WORLD
(1907)

Many people would be surprised to learn that *The Playboy of the Western World* is not about dashing young men with brilliantined hair; neither is it set in Monte Carlo or Biarritz. Its plot, instead, is as follows (as summarized by an unsympathetic reviewer in the Dublin *Freeman's Journal* of February 2, 1907):

> A broken-down, evil-looking tramp enters a low public-house on the coast of Mayo, and after some inquiry admits to those gathered there that he has murdered his father. The doubting, mistrustful attitude of his hearers at once changes into one of awe and admiration. He is installed as pot-boy at the request of the publican's daughter, and is left in charge of the shebeen by the father.
>
> In the second act we are shown the countryside flocking to pay homage to the man who, in the language of the dramatist, has 'killed his da'. The women are depicted wooing with no trace of modesty this delightful type of strong, passionate man. Pegeen-Mike, the publican's daughter, jilts her timid betrothed for him. Ultimately, however, the supposed murdered parent turns up, and recognises his son, whose popularity then declines as a natural consequence.

The play is thus a story of Irish peasant life. The 'playboy' – slang of the day for a champion or sportsman – is a poor farmer, Christy Mahon, who boasts that he has killed his father by striking him with a 'loy' (a spade). The 'Western World' is the rugged and backward west of Ireland.

During the composition of the play Synge made several attempts at a title – among them *The Fool of Farnham*, *The Murderer (A Farce)* and *Murder Will Out, or, The Fool of the Family* – before arriving at his final choice. The very different title *The Playboy of the Western World* was of great significance to the reception of the play and his own career. The reasons were largely political.

In 1907, in the period before the creation of the Irish Free State, the whole of the island of Ireland was under the control of the English. The nationalist movement was flexing its muscles – it was the period immediately before the Easter Rising of 1916. The Dublin Abbey Theatre, home of the 'National Theatre' of Ireland, was a forum for debate on the meaning of Irishness and the practicability of home rule. Founded in 1904 as an offshoot of the Irish Literary Theatre, the Abbey had staged plays by W.B. Yeats, J.M. Synge, Lady Gregory, A.E., Oliver St John Gogarty and Thomas MacDonagh. It was seen as key to the Irish Literary Revival.

In this context, when *The Playboy*, with its low characters, disturbing violence and glorification of parricide, received its première at the Abbey in February 1907, it was seen in some quarters as a treacherous attack on Irishness itself, and particularly on the ordinary Catholic peasantry of the rural West. What happened next has come to be known as 'the Playboy riots'.

THE ABBEY THEATRE
UPROARIOUS SCENES
PROTESTS AGAINST MR SYNGE'S PLAY
SPEECH OF MR W.G. FAY
THE POLICE CALLED IN.
POLICE ACTED IN DUMB SHOW.

The *Irish Independent* described events on opening night as the play approached its second act:

> The act went on, but not a soul in the place heard a word, so great was the din created by the folk in the gallery.
>
> The latter sang songs, hissed, called the policemen names, denounced the players, invited the author to a free fight, and before the act was over the curtain went down amidst terrific hissing and boohing. There were again cries for the author, but he did not come forward; and Mr. Fay, coming to the footlights, said something which was not audible, and the curtain went down again amidst cheers.
>
> At this juncture Lady Gregory and the author of the play entered the auditorium, and there were again cries for the author's speech. Mr. Synge, who took his seat near the orchestra, when asked by a reporter if he would say anything, replied that he was suffering from influenza, and could not speak; and owing to the rigorous cries of the audience he was obliged to leave the auditorium.
>
> The final act was then proceeded with, but no one in the house heard a word of it owing to the din created by the audience, many of whom cried – 'Sinn Fein'; 'Sinn Fein Amhain' and 'Kill the Author'.

The audience was in no doubt that 'the Western World' referred specifically to the Western counties of Ireland. As the *Evening Mail* reported, during the disturbances 'someone called out "That's not Western life". At the close of this act a burly young fellow in the front of the pit started to sing in lusty tones, "The Men of the West", and the chorus was taken up by those around him.' Letters in the newspapers in subsequent days included comments such as the following, from 'A

Western Girl': 'I am well acquainted with the conditions of life in the West, and not only does this play not truly represent these conditions, but it portrays the people of that part of Ireland as a coarse, besotted race, without one gleam of genuine humour or one sparkle of virtue.'

It is difficult to see the use of 'Western' in the title as anything other than a piece of deliberate provocation by Synge. It raised the stakes significantly, pointing a finger straight at the salt-of-the-earth stereotype of rural Ireland which was so dear to the heart of the growing nationalist movement.

As in many later controversies, the play was attacked by people who had obviously never seen it. One reviewer spoke of 'a vile and inhuman story told in the foulest language we have ever listened to from a public platform'. Apart from a couple of 'bloodies' there is in fact nothing offensive in the language of the play, and the sexual content is muted even by 1907 standards. But perhaps the reviewer had been unable to hear the actors. During every performance the audience had drowned out the dialogue. Unrest only died down when the play was taken off, after one week. The riots spelled the end of Synge's career in Ireland: the Abbey Theatre decided not to risk staging his next play, *The Tinker's Wedding*, his last completed work. He died in 1909.

The Playboy of the Western World therefore has some interesting resonances. It is not difficult to think of recent works where the title alone has been enough to damn them. Neither are calls for authors to be killed very uncommon. Synge, by crafting such an incendiary play, with such an incendiary title, knew he was playing with fire. Like others that came after him, he probably didn't realize how badly he'd be burned.

28. MARRIED LOVE
(1918)

Marie Stopes was the twentieth century's most influential British thinker on sex. In her pioneering work *Married Love* she attempted to give guidelines on how 'to increase the joys of marriage, and show how much sorrow may be avoided', achieving this end through realistic descriptions of the sexual act and discussion of things such as contraception, orgasm and artificial insemination. She would have hated the idea, but with *Married Love* she gave a long, energetic push to the twentieth-century sexual juggernaut. It is partly because of her work that, for example, gay rights and abortion clinics – things she would have been appalled by – later became familiar features of Western sexual culture.

In *Married Love* she also had a confession to make. 'In my own marriage I paid such a terrible price for sex-ignorance that I feel that knowledge gained at such a cost should be put at the service of humanity.' She was referring to her marriage to the geneticist Reginald Ruggles Gates in 1911, annulled on grounds of non-consummation in 1916. A certificate she had obtained from her family doctor attested that 'There is evidence from the condition of the hymen that there has not been penetration by a normal male organ.' It proved the clinching piece of evidence in court. Asked to confirm that this was the case, Marie said: 'On hundreds of occasions on which we had what I thought were relations, I only remember three occasions on which it was partially rigid, and then it was never effectively rigid.' An interjection by Mr Justice Sherman drove the point home: 'He never succeeded in penetrating into your private parts?' 'No,' Marie replied. The petition was granted.

Between the annulment and the publication of *Married Love* she remained unmarried and did not conduct any love affair. When, therefore, she published *Married Love*, a book about sex, she had, by her own testimony, never actually experienced sex. Strangely enough, this was an advantage, not a drawback.

Her public status as a virgin rather titillated the book-buying public. Marie was young and attractive, and a wronged woman. The story of her struggles in court to detach herself from an impotent husband added immeasurably to the *frisson* of the book. Perhaps more importantly, her virginity helped to deflect any charges of immorality that such an explicit guide would normally have attracted. *Married Love* was shocking. There was a risk of prosecution for obscenity: other campaigners had been prosecuted before her. But Marie's virginity was a foil to the shocks she was administering. Her own purity was set as a counterbalance to what might be perceived as her wantonness. The fact that she was not prosecuted for obscenity, the fact that she remained miraculously untouchable, was due partly to the fact that she had never been touched.

The title *Married Love* was crucial in much the same way. It was not her first choice. In manuscript it had been *They Twain*, and the book had been conceived as a romantic novel. These origins can still be glimpsed in the final text ('The half-swooning sense of flux which overtakes the spirit in that eternal moment at the apex of rapture sweeps into its flaming tides the essence of the man and the woman . . .'). But as Marie wrote and rewrote it, gradually drawing away from the initial concept and towards the idea of a matter-of-fact sex manual, she realized that she needed to make it clear that the book was not a salacious piece of pulp fiction but a respectable guide for the monogamous married. If there was discussion of sex, it had to be married sex. 'Sex', of course, could not be in the title: the Edwardian euphemism 'love' would stand in for it. Clear, simple, demure and yet paradoxically rather suggestive, *Married Love* was perfect. Partly as a result of the title, the book survived prosecution, sold in its millions and became probably the most sexually influential tract of the twentieth century.

The question remains, though: did Reginald's parts ever get 'effectively rigid'? Was Marie a virgin in 1916? She certainly had powerful personal reasons for wishing to be one. Her relationship with Gates had broken down and she desperately wanted a divorce. As the law stood, the plea of non-consummation was the only one open to her. The retention of her hymen after 1916, whether in fiction or in fact, was thus the only way she could escape wedlock. It also enabled her to continue to cherish the idea of the unique monogamous pair-bond as the centre of her sexual idealism. Without a hymen, she was a failure in the lists of marriage; with one, she could start again. Without one, the fault was hers; with one, the fault was Gates's. The transference of power was total. As she wrote to Gates's father, explaining the affair: 'Reginald has failed me in almost every way possible for a husband to fail.'

But important evidence also comes from Gates's side of the case. He kept his own account of the divorce suit, which his second wife deposited in the British Library after his death. It does not bear out Marie's version:

At our first sexual congress she had twitted me with having had no sexual experience. This was true. Although I had been greatly tempted many times, I had managed to lead a celibate life as a result of my strict religious upbringing combined with hard scientific work. I was probably clumsy at first, through lack of experience, but we were soon having intercourse frequently enough to satisfy a normal woman . . . The use of contraceptives, however, detracted from the joy of these experiences for me and doubtless acted as an impeding factor in my own sexual activity.

Further testimony, perhaps unconscious, came from Marie herself. In *Married Love*, written, it was claimed, while still a virgin, she shows a great deal of familiarity with the rude mechanics of domestic sex. It is hard to believe that the following passages on the coital aftermath were culled from consultations in the British Library reading room:

> Then, when the propitious hour arrives, and after the love-play, the growing passion expands, until the transports of feeling find their ending in the explosive completion of the act, at once the tension of his whole system relaxes, and his muscles fall into gentle, easy attitudes of languorous content, and in a few moments the man is sleeping like a child.
>
> [...] when a wife is left sleepless through the neglect of the mate who slumbers healthily by her side, it is not surprising if she spends the long hours reviewing their mutual position; and the review cannot yield her much pleasure or satisfaction. For deprived of the physical delight of mutual orgasm (though, perhaps, like so many wives, quite unconscious of all it can give), she sees in the sex act an arrangement where pleasure, relief and subsequent sleep, are all on her husband's side, while she is left merely the passive instrument of his enjoyment.

Marie often extrapolated from her own personal experience to the general rule. These descriptions of a 'wham, bam, thank you ma'am' encounter are sufficiently detailed to be plausibly autobiographical. It seems more likely that Gates's crime was not giving her an orgasm.

There remains the question of the virginity certificate. It supports her case, but it is hardly emphatic. 'There is evidence', it states cautiously, 'that there has not been penetration by a normal male organ.' But, as Marie may have been aware, the hymen can and sometimes does partially survive intercourse. Penetration by some sort of organ could still have taken place. And in fact, Gates's own doctor, Sir Alfred Fripp, later examined the organ in question and gave it its own counter-certificate of 'perfect normality'.

Did Dr Marie Stopes experience 'married love' before 1916? Whatever the truth, it was undoubtedly her experience of marriage to Gates that gave her the motivation for her book. As a marriage, the Stopes–Gates connection failed. It had a child, however: *Married Love*. And that succeeded beyond anyone's expectations.

29. MY MAN JEEVES
(1919)

Had it been summer, he would have taken some literature out on to the cricket-field or the downs, and put in
a little steady reading there, with the aid of a bag of
cherries.

P.G. Wodehouse, *The Gold Bat* (1904)

My Man Jeeves (1919) was the first Wodehouse book with
Jeeves in the title. There were ten more: *The Inimitable Jeeves*
(1923), *Carry On, Jeeves* (1925), *Very Good, Jeeves* (1930),
Thank You, Jeeves (1934), *Right Ho, Jeeves* (1934), *Ring for
Jeeves* (1953), *Jeeves and the Feudal Spirit* (1954), *Jeeves in
the Offing* (1960), *Stiff Upper Lip, Jeeves* (1963) and *Much
Obliged, Jeeves* (1971). In addition there were a number of
US editions with alternative 'Jeeves' titles, such as *The Return
of Jeeves* (1953) and *How Right You Are, Jeeves* (1960), and
several novels or story collections about Jeeves and Bertie but
without Jeeves in the title (such as *The Mating Season*, 1949).

Although *My Man Jeeves* was the first Jeeves title, Jeeves
the gentleman's personal gentleman – he of the head that
sticks out at the back, possessor of the secret of how to make
a perfect cup of tea and serve it precisely as his master is
waking up – himself first made an appearance in the story
'Extricating Young Gussie' in the *Saturday Evening Post* of
September 18, 1915. He had only two lines: 'Mrs Gregson to
see you, sir' and 'Very good, sir. Which suit will you wear?'
Wodehouse said in the introduction to the anthology *The
World of Jeeves* (1967): 'It was only some time later, when I
was going into the strange affair of The Artistic Career of
Corky, that the man's qualities dawned upon me. I still blush

to think of the off-hand way I treated him at our first encounter.' 'The Artistic Career of Corky' was in fact a later title for the story 'Leave it to Jeeves', which appeared in the *Saturday Evening Post* of February 5, 1916. In it Jeeves shimmers into the plot in a fully fledged Jeeves-like manner, and sets about helping Bertie's artistic pal Corky out of a fiancée-related jam. On the way he does several other things that became later Jeeves stock-in-trades, such as disapproving of Bertie's suiting arrangements and dispensing racing tips.

One more tale deserves mention, one which has misled some into thinking it features the debut of Jeeves. This is 'Jeeves Takes Charge', a short story published, again in the *Saturday Evening Post*, on November 18, 1916, more than a year after 'Extricating Young Gussie'. Bertie has discovered his regular valet in the act of stealing his silk socks, and has reluctantly been forced to hand him the mitten. The agency then sends a new man:

> 'If you would drink this, sir,' he said, with a kind of bedside manner, rather like the royal doctor shooting the bracer into the sick prince. 'It is a little preparation of my own invention. It is the Worcester Sauce that gives it its colour. The raw egg makes it nutritious. The red pepper gives it its bite. Gentlemen have told me they have found it extremely invigorating after a late evening.' [...]
>
> 'You're engaged!' I said, as soon as I could say anything.
>
> I perceived clearly that this cove was one of the world's wonders, the sort no home should be without.
>
> 'Thank you, sir. My name is Jeeves.'

Jeeves, then, was born in 1915 or thereabouts – during the first battles of the First World War. Wodehouse was working in the New York theatre at the time, having been living in the

USA on and off since about 1909. Before he left permanently for America, however, he went to a cricket match in Cheltenham. And this was where war, cricket and Jeeves met and coalesced.

Percy Jeeves was, by all accounts, a very useful player. Born in 1888, in Earlsheaton, Yorkshire, he played for Goole and then Hawes cricket clubs before signing up for the Warwickshire County side. An attacking right-hand bat, right-arm medium-fast bowler, he played first-class cricket from 1912 to 1914. 1913 was the season when he really began to distinguish himself, taking 106 wickets and scoring 785 runs. It was also the year in which Wodehouse, a keen cricket fan,[1] saw him play at Cheltenham. Several decades later, R.V. Ryder, the son of the Warwickshire club secretary who had originally signed Percy Jeeves, wrote to Wodehouse to ask for confirmation that the Jeeves of literature really was named after the Jeeves of cricket. Wodehouse replied:

Dear Mr Ryder.

Yes, you are quite right.

It must have been in 1913 that I paid a visit to my parents in Cheltenham and went to see Warwickshire play Glos on the Cheltenham College ground. I suppose Jeeves's bowling must have impressed me, for I remembered him in 1916,[2] when I was in New York and just starting the Jeeves and Bertie saga, and it was just the name I wanted.

I have always thought till lately that he was playing for Gloucestershire that day. (I remember admiring his action very much)

Yours sincerely,

P.G. Wodehouse.[3]

Percy Jeeves went on to even greater distinction in the 1914 season, and was tipped by England captain Plum Warner as a future England player.

On August 4, 1914, however, Britain declared war on Germany, and Jeeves signed up with the 15th Battalion of the Royal Warwickshire Regiment. In July the following year he was in the thick of the fighting in the battle of the Somme. The 15th Battalion was ordered to make an attack on High Wood, a forested area on the crest of a hill near the village of Bazentin le Petit in the Somme *département*. High Wood was a crucial part of the German line, and heavily defended with machine-gun emplacements able to rake down the slopes at every approach. The ground between the British trenches and the hilltop was open, unforested and strewn with dead bodies from previous actions. On the night of July 22/23 the order was given for a major assault, in which the 15th Battalion was a small component. The assault made no headway whatever. Jeeves's body was never found. It was only in September 1915 that High Wood was captured, after the loss of around 6,000 men.

September 1915 was also, coincidentally, the month of the appearance of the first Jeeves story. Jeeves never got to play for his country, but did die for it.

---

1 There are numerous cricket-related stories from Wodehouse's early writing. One of the novels is *The Gold Bat* (1904), a school story revolving around the theft of a cricketing trophy in the form of a miniature golden bat, quoted from above.

2 Wodehouse mistook the date of the first appearance of the fictional Jeeves, which was in 1915.

3 The original letter is in the Edgbaston Cricket Ground museum.

30. ULYSSES
(1922)

I managed to get my copy of *Ulysses* through safely this time. I rather wish I had never read it. It gives me an inferiority complex. When I read a book like that and then come back to my own work, I feel like a eunuch who has taken a course in voice production.

George Orwell, letter to Brenda Salkeld, 1933

In 2006 the poet laureate Andrew Motion recommended that all schoolchildren read *Ulysses* as part of their essential grounding in English literature. One can see why. To read *Ulysses* is to realize that the whole of twentieth-century literature is little more than a James Joyce Appreciation Society. Among the many writers who would have been different, or even nonexistent, without *Ulysses* are Samuel Beckett, Dylan Thomas, Flann O'Brien, Anthony Burgess, Salman Rushdie, Umberto Eco, Italo Calvino, Philip K. Dick and Bernard Malamud (to name but a few). Even a writer as unlikely as George Orwell deliberately echoed the 'Circe' episode of *Ulysses* in the play scene of *A Clergyman's Daughter*. Joyce's hectic layering of styles, his unstoppable neologizing, his blurring of viewpoint, his love of parody and imitation, his obscenity, his difficulty, obscurity and outright incomprehensibility was the beginning of the high modernist style in world literature. Andrew Motion was right in seeing *Ulysses* as fundamental. But in another way his suggestion was absurd. *Ulysses* is not a book for children. It is barely even a book for adults. The paradox of *Ulysses* is that one needs to read it to understand twentieth-century literature, but one needs to read twentieth-century literature to build up the stamina to read *Ulysses*.

The problem starts with the title. Early readers of *Ulysses*, exhilarated and appalled after 800 pages, were often still left thinking 'Why Ulysses?' Ulysses is barely mentioned.[1] The solution, as we now know, after a century's worth of scholarly investigation and Joyce's own prompting, is that the book is an intricate allegory of the *Odyssey* (the hero being latinized from Odysseus to Ulysses). *Ulysses* is divided into eighteen parts, or 'episodes' as Joyce scholars call them, each written in a different style and with a different Odyssean name, though the names themselves are not given in the text. The names are: Telemachus, Nestor, Proteus, Calypso, Lotus Eaters, Hades, Aeolus, Lestrygonians, Scylla and Charybdis, Wandering Rocks, Sirens, Cyclops, Nausicaa, Oxen of the Sun, Circe, Eumaeus, Ithaca and Penelope. Each episode is assigned, tacitly, a colour theme, a dominant organ of the body, an hour, a setting and other characteristics, though many of these remain a matter of scholarly dispute.[2] The action takes place in Dublin on a single June day (June 14, 1904) and its three main characters are Leopold Bloom, Stephen Dedalus and Molly Bloom, who represent Ulysses, Telemachus and Penelope. Other characters and places also have their Homeric counterparts.

The problem is that one can know all of this and still be left thinking 'Why Ulysses?' The choice of the *Odyssey* seems somewhat arbitrary. Why not *Oedipus Rex* as a background text? That way Bloom could be Oedipus, Molly Jocasta and Dedalus Tiresias (or someone else). *Ulysses* is not so much a novel as a symbolic system, rather like a clock or a computer programme. Underlying the final, visible product, the time-telling or the computer display, is a corresponding machinery, the cogs or the binary code. Why did Joyce choose the *Odyssey* for his code?

The answer is that it could hardly have been anything else. Joyce was from an early age deeply in love with the *Odyssey*. 'The character of Ulysses has fascinated me ever since boyhood,' he wrote to Carlo Linati in 1920. As a schoolboy he read

Charles Lamb's *Adventures of Ulysses*, an adventure-yarn version of the story which presents, in Lamb's words, 'a brave man struggling with adversity; by a wise use of events, and with an inimitable presence of mind under difficulties, forcing out a way for himself.' Joyce said later that the story so gripped him that when at Belvedere College (he would have been between the ages of eleven and fifteen) he was tasked to write an essay on 'My Favourite Hero', he chose Ulysses.[3] He later described Ulysses to Frank Budgeon as the only 'complete all-round character presented by any writer . . . a complete man . . . a good man'.

Unsurprisingly therefore, this 'complete man' surfaced as early as Joyce's first major prose work: *Dubliners* of 1914. Joyce had originally planned that it include a short story called 'Ulysses', the plot of which was based on an incident which took place in June 1904. Joyce was involved in a scuffle on St Stephen's Green, Dublin, after accosting another man's lady-companion, and was rescued and patched up by one Albert H. Hunter. Hunter, according to Joyce's biographer, Richard Ellmann, was 'rumoured to be Jewish and to have an unfaithful wife' (in both of these respects a prototype for Leopold Bloom). In 1906 Joyce wrote to his brother Stanislaus: 'I have a new story for *Dubliners* in my head. It deals with Mr Hunter.' In a letter written shortly afterwards he mentioned its title: 'I thought of beginning my story *Ulysses* but I have too many cares at present.' Three months later he had abandoned the idea, writing: '*Ulysses* never got any forrader than its title.' The incident with Hunter was only written up later, in *Ulysses* itself, in a passage at the end of episode fifteen in which Bloom rescues Dedalus 'in orthodox Samaritan fashion' from a fight. The idea of Ulysses as symbolic hero – and as a title – was therefore present as early as 1906. Its centrality to the early plan for *Dubliners* was revealed in a conversation with Georges Borach:

When I was writing *Dubliners*, I first wished to choose the title *Ulysses in Dublin*, but gave up the idea. In Rome, when I had finished about half of the *Portrait*, I realized that the *Odyssey* had to be the sequel, and I began to write *Ulysses*.

The figure of Ulysses could not therefore have been less arbitrary. He existed as a thread through all of Joyce's prose works from 'My Favourite Hero' onward. He was there in embryo in *Dubliners*, was being considered halfway through *Portrait of the Artist as a Young Man*, and burst out in his full, final and inevitable form in the work that bore his name. It was only after publication of *Ulysses* in 1922 that Joyce was free of his 'favourite hero', and could allow his literature to expand to its ultimate extent. The book that came after *Ulysses* was *Finnegans Wake*, a work not tied to one hero but inclusive of all heroes, not tied to one myth but including all myths, and using not one language but all languages.

1 The name is mentioned four times, twice in passing as a proper name (Ulysses Grant and Ulysses Browne) and twice as a brief mention among other heroes and notables. David Lodge in *The Art of Fiction* wrote that the title, as a clue to the allegorical nature of the book, was 'the only absolutely unmissable one in the entire text'.

2 Scholars were egged on by Joyce's own frequent hints. He wrote to Carlo Linati in 1920: 'It is the epic of two races (Israel–Ireland) and at the same time the cycle of the human body as well as a little story of a day (life) . . . It is also a kind of encyclopaedia. My intention is not only to render the myth *sub specie temporis nostri* but also to allow each adventure (that is, every hour, every organ, every art being interconnected and interrelated in the somatic scheme of the whole) to condition and even to create its own technique. Each adventure is so to speak one person although it is composed of persons – as Aquinas relates of the heavenly hosts.'

3 The essay title 'My Favourite Hero' actually appears in *Ulysses*, on page 638 of the World's Classics edition.

31. THE WASTE LAND
(1922)

The Waste Land begins (of course):

> April is the cruellest month, breeding
> Lilacs out of the dead land, mixing
> Memory and desire, stirring
> Dull roots with spring rain.

Not so in the first version:

> First we had a couple of feelers down at Tom's place,
> There was old Tom, boiled to the eyes, blind
> (Don't you remember that time after a dance,
> Top hats and all, we and Silk Hat Harry,
> And old Tom took us behind, brought out a bottle of fizz . . .

The transformation occurred in January 1921. Eliot met Ezra Pound in Paris and showed him a draft of a long poem he had written in the course of the previous few months. It was called 'He Do the Police in Different Voices', and was the proto-*Waste Land*. It took its title from a passage in Dickens's *Our Mutual Friend*, in which 'Sloppy' (a young man so named because he had been found in the street on a 'sloppy' night) is praised by Betty for his skill at reading:

> 'For I ain't, you must know,' said Betty, 'much of a hand at reading writing-hand, though I can read my Bible and most print. And I do love a newspaper. You mightn't think it, but Sloppy is a beautiful reader of a newspaper. He do the Police in different voices.'

Pound, given the job of editor, did not feel at all intimidated. He laid about him with gusto, slashing through page after page, reducing the poem in size almost by half. He cut away the embarrassing scenes above, of a drunken spree in Boston with old Tom and Silk Hat Harry; he cut 27 lines on the further adventures of the typist and the young man carbuncular; a further 160 lines dealing with the doings of Fresca and Phlebas; and junked 84 lines of part IV, making it the shortest of the five parts. He also made around 200 suggestions and emendations. By the time he had finished, the poem was radically different. In Pound's version the poem began with the prophetic voice of Tiresias ('April is the cruellest month...'), and this voice went on to dominate the poem. Gone was the archness, the vaudevillian scenes of lowlife, the period-piece flavour. 'He Do the Police in Different Voices', which had originally been chosen – apologetically? – to suggest a miscellany of voices, was now not quite so accurate. The poem had gained structure.

Casting around for a title for his new poem, Eliot settled on 'The Waste Land', and the poem was published as such in *The Criterion* in October 1922 (and later as a small book). He wrote in a prefatory note: 'Not only the title, but the plan and a good deal of the incidental symbolism of the poem were suggested by Miss Jessie L. Weston's book on the Grail legend: *From Ritual to Romance* (Macmillan).'

From Ritual to Romance was the *Da Vinci Code* of the 1920s. Its argument was that the legend of the Holy Grail had roots in very ancient myths dealing with a Fisher King who had suffered a wound – in many versions a sexual wound – which had affected the fertility of the land. The king awaited a hero who would heal him: meanwhile he was kept alive by the power of the grail, and spent his time fishing. These myths had been overlaid by later Christian symbolism, and their origins perhaps deliberately hushed up. Weston made it clear that the symbol of the 'Waste Land' was central to her book:

> As a matter of fact I believe that the 'Waste Land' is really the very heart of our problem; a rightful appreciation of its position and significance will place us in possession of the clue which will lead us safely through the most bewildering mazes of the fully developed tale.

Among the 'incidental symbolism' Eliot took from Weston was the Fisher King, the tarot pack, the desert land where there is no water, the myths of Phoenician origin. Of course, there is more to *The Waste Land* than this. Without Weston there would still have been Stetson and his corpse, that Shakespeherian Rag, Mr Eugenides, Elizabeth and Leicester, the broken fingernails of dirty hands, Datta, Dayadhvam, Damyata. But Eliot did fairly when he credited Weston as a major influence, naming his poem after the main theme of her book.

Unless . . .

In 1913 Madison Cawein, a poet from Louisville, Kentucky, published a poem in the Chicago magazine *Poetry*. It was called 'Waste Land'.

Waste Land

> Briar and fennel and chincapin,
>   And rue and ragweed everywhere;
> The field seemed sick as a soul with sin,
>   Or dead of an old despair,
>   Born of an ancient care.
>
> The cricket's cry and the locust's whirr,
>   And the note of a bird's distress,

With the rasping sound of the grasshopper,
    Clung to the loneliness
    Like burrs to a trailing dress.

So sad the field, so waste the ground,
    So curst with an old despair,
A woodchuck's burrow, a blind mole's mound,
    And a chipmunk's stony lair,
    Seemed more than it could bear.

So lonely, too, so more than sad,
    So droning-lone with bees –
I wondered what more could Nature add
    To the sum of its miseries . . .
    And then – I saw the trees.

Skeletons gaunt that gnarled the place,
    Twisted and torn they rose –
The tortured bones of a perished race
    Of monsters no mortal knows,
    They startled the mind's repose.

And a man stood there, as still as moss,
    A lichen form that stared;
With an old blind hound that, at a loss,
    Forever around him fared
    With a snarling fang half bared.

I looked at the man; I saw him plain;
    Like a dead weed, gray and wan,
Or a breath of dust. I looked again –
    And man and dog were gone,
    Like wisps of the graying dawn . . .

> Were they a part of the grim death there –
>   Ragweed, fennel, and rue?
> Or forms of the mind, an old despair,
>   That there into semblance grew
>   Out of the grief I knew?

Eliot could easily have read it. Ezra Pound was *Poetry*'s European editor, and in the same issue had written a piece on 'Poets now in London' (though without mentioning Eliot: they didn't meet until 1914). Cawein's poem was introduced with the comment that its author was 'too well known to need any introduction'.

One sees immediately that Cawein's 'Waste Land' is very different in style from Eliot's *The Waste Land*. It reads like a work of late-Victorian origin, perhaps a minor work by Hardy. The fifth line of every stanza never really works. But the correspondences with *The Waste Land* are startling. The critic Robert Ian Scott, writing in *The Times Literary Supplement* in 1995, noted at least thirteen similarities, including the title and basic theme (that of a cursed land), with images of crying crickets, notes of a bird, stony ground, dust, dead trees, a dog and a disappearing man. Scott went on to suggest that Eliot had reasons for hiding his debt to Cawein: 'Had Eliot or his advocates mentioned Madison Cawein, the poet laureate of Louisville, alongside the Bible, Dante and Shakespeare, his own poem might have seemed a hoax or joke, and much less original. None the less, Cawein seems to have provided the emotional geography on which Eliot's poem, its effect and much of his fame are based.'

But *The Waste Land* is not a plagiarized 'Waste Land', and the argument smacks rather of a conspiracy theory, requiring that Eliot square things with his 'advocates' and the literary establishment. True, there are dogs in both poems, but there is not much resemblance between Cawein's 'old blind hound' and Eliot's 'O keep the dog far hence, that's friend to men' (this is the only dog in *The Waste Land*, not counting the Isle of Dogs). There is 'stony' ground in both poems, but there is no seemingly direct line of transmission between Cawein's 'chipmunk's stony lair' and Eliot's evocation of the Passion – 'the agony in stony places'. The most that can be said, it seems, is that Cawein may have been one influence among many in the scraps and jottings Eliot presented to Pound as 'He Do the Police in Different Voices'. The title 'The Waste Land', it must be remembered, was an afterthought. It is conceivable that Eliot was remembering Cawein's 1913 poem in 1922 as he retitled his poem, but it is not the likeliest theory. Neither does Cawein's 'emotional geography' seem too close to Eliot's. The emotion of *The Waste Land* is Eliot's own, as he sat down in Margate and Lausanne in 1920, ill, depressed and worried about his failing marriage.[1] It is a poem, above all, about Eliot. The voice we hear when we read it is not Cawein's, just as it is not Weston's. Nor, for that matter, is it Pound's, Baudelaire's, Webster's, Pope's, Donne's, Shakespeare's, the Buddha's, Goldsmith's, Dante's, Isaiah's, Wagner's or Milton's. It is T.S. Eliot's voice, and it is one of the most distinctive in all literature:

> In this decayed hole among the mountains
> In the faint moonlight, the grass is singing
> Over the tumbled graves, about the chapel
> There is the empty chapel, only the wind's home.

1 In the introduction to her publication of his letters, Valerie Eliot (Eliot's second wife) quotes Eliot as saying that: 'To her [Vivienne, his first wife], the marriage brought no happiness, to me, it brought the state of mind out of which came *The Waste Land*.'

32. THE EGO AND THE ID
(1923)

Freud had something of a genius for titles. *The Psychopathology of Everyday Life* is startling and witty; *Beyond the Pleasure Principle* is intriguing and titillating. *The Ego and the Id* demonstrates the same mastery. With all the confidence of his forty clinical years, Freud introduced in his title a completely new term, the 'Id'.

Although it wasn't *quite* new. A couple of weeks previously, another book had appeared: *The Book of the It*. The author was the analyst George Groddeck. Both Freud and Groddeck used the same German term for their 'Id' and 'It' respectively: *das Es*. Freud was quite open about his debt: rather shockingly, he announced that *The Ego and the Id* was 'under the sponsorship of Groddeck'. It was shocking because Groddeck was regarded in some quarters as little better than a lunatic.

In the early years of psychoanalysis, practitioners were very anxious to establish their respectability as legitimate medical men. This was still an age of sexual puritanism, in which the sexual organs and sexual functions were not generally mentioned in polite conversation, and in which sexual categories as we now know them, or think we know them – homosexuality, bisexuality, transvestism, transsexualism – were still at an early and controversial stage of development. In this atmosphere, George Groddeck delivered a notorious speech to the congress of psychoanalysts at The Hague in 1920, opening his address with the words: 'I am a wild analyst.' This was somewhat crass. Analysts were regarded by the public as 'wild' already: it was exactly the image the profession wished to avoid. In his speech Groddeck went on to develop the idea that unconscious forces were the rulers of the human organism: even bodily diseases were caused by unconscious conflicts and neuroses, which meant, in broad terms, that you could cure, say, an ovarian cyst, by talking to your patient. Groddeck moreover insisted on bringing his mistress to conferences and was the author of a risqué novel, *The Seeker of Souls*. The analyst Oskar Pfister wrote to Freud that he liked 'fresh butter' and that 'Groddeck very often reminds me of rancid butter.'

Nevertheless Freud liked Groddeck personally. He wrote to Max Eitingon that Groddeck was 'a bit of a fantasist, but an original fellow who has the rare gift of good humour. I should not like to do without him.' And Freud and Groddeck were in regular correspondence about their projects in 1923. Groddeck was working on what would become *The Book of the It*, a book which, characteristically, was not so much a work of psychoanalysis as a mixture of scientific treatise, epistolary novel and confessional. It was couched in the form of a series of letters from a man to a woman, and central to the book was the concept of the It. Groddeck wrote to Freud:

> I am of the opinion that man is animated by the unknown. There is an It in him, something marvellous that regulates everything that he does and that happens to him. The sentence 'I live' is only partially correct; it expresses a little partial phenomenon of the fundamental truth: 'Man is lived by the It.'

Groddeck sent Freud the chapters as he completed them, and Freud sent back letters of encouragement, also revealing the direction of his own thinking on the composition of the psyche. Taking Groddeck's idea of the It, along with previous notions of the unconscious, as well as other speculations on the nature of personality, Freud was crafting the model that came to dominate psychiatry in the twentieth century. This was the tripartite model of Ego, Id and Superego, which he set out for the first time in the book *The Ego and the Id*.

This model is most easily explained in the way Freud himself explained it in the book, as a horse and rider. The Ego 'resembles the rider who is supposed to rein in the superior strength of the horse, with the difference that the rider does this with his own, the Ego with borrowed strength.' The Ego thinks it is in charge, but in reality is pulled this way and that by the powerful sex and death drives of the horse/Id: the Ego is 'accustomed to translating the will of the Id into action as if that will were its own'. In the meantime, the Ego has another problem to contend with: the Superego, which might be envisaged as a small thundercloud hovering above the rider's head. The Superego is conscience, the voice of the father, moral pressure. The Superego and the Id explicitly gang up on the Ego: 'The Superego is always in close touch with the Id and can act as its representative in relation to the Ego.'

It is important to look at the actual terms Freud used. In German the title of his book was *Das Ich und das Es* (The I and the It).[1] It was only in the Standard Edition of Freud's works in English that the latinate Ego, Id and Superego were used. Freud's Id was therefore, as already mentioned, terminologically identical with Groddeck's It in *The Book of the It* (in German *Das Buch vom Es*). But in analytical practice there were some important differences between It and Id. For Freud, the Ego, although largely controlled by the Id, was in some senses an agency: it had limited powers of will, despite its unhappy position at the centre of pressures from the Id, the Superego, and the external world. For Groddeck, the psyche had no conscious agency at all. The unconscious It regulated everything.

Some time after the publication of both books, on the occasion of Groddeck's sixtieth birthday, Freud sent him a letter with his best wishes, in a form which neatly encapsulated his debt. It was as if the elements of Freud's psyche were wishing happy birthday to the single hidden force of Groddeck's: 'My Ego and my Id congratulate your It.'

1 The term Superego in the book was *das Über-Ich* (the Over-I).

33. THE GREAT GATSBY
(1925)

Fitzgerald agonized over the title of his third novel. Among the candidates he rejected, and then lighted on again, and then re-rejected, in a series of letters and telegrams to his editor Max Perkins, were *Trimalchio*, *Trimalchio's Banquet*, *Among the Ash Heaps and Millionaires*, *The High-Bouncing Lover*, *The Great Gatsby*, *Gold-Hatted Gatsby*, *Gatsby*, *On the Road to West Egg*, *Incident at West Egg*, *Trimalchio in West Egg* and several others. Perkins steered him gently towards *The Great Gatsby*, despite Fitzgerald's doubts.

By the time *The Great Gatsby* was at the printers, Fitzgerald had changed his mind once again, asking Perkins for the book to be retitled *Under the Red, White and Blue* – a reference to the American Dream so horribly mutilated in the book – and continued to swing back and forth, later writing to Perkins: 'I feel *Trimalchio* might have been best after all', but by then it was in the bookshops. *The Great Gatsby* it had to stay.

Why Gatsby? It is not a common name, and Fitzgerald was careful with names. A celebrated passage listing the revellers at Gatsby's parties reads as follows:

> From East Egg, then, came the Chester Beckers and the Leeches and a man named Bunsen whom I knew at Yale and Doctor Webster Civet who was drowned last summer up in Maine. And the Hornbeams and the Willie Voltaires and a whole clan named Blackbuck who always gathered in a corner and flipped up their noses like goats at whosoever came near [. . .]
>
> Clarence Endive was from East Egg, as I remember. He came only once, in white knickerbockers, and had a

fight with a bum named Etty in the garden. From farther out on the Island came the Cheadles and the O.R.P. Schraeders and the Stonewall Jackson Abrams of Georgia and the Fishguards and the Ripley Snells. Snell was there three days before he went to the penitentiary, so drunk out on the gravel drive that Mrs. Ulysses Swett's automobile ran over his right hand. The Dancies came too and S. B. Whitebait, who was well over sixty, and Maurice A. Flink and the Hammerheads and Beluga the tobacco importer and Beluga's girls.

From West Egg came the Poles and the Mulreadys and Cecil Roebuck [. . .] And the Catlips and the Bembergs and G. Earl Muldoon, brother to that Muldoon who afterwards strangled his wife. Da Fontano the promoter came there and Ed Legros and James B. ('Rot-gut') Ferret and the de Jongs and Ernest Lilly . . .

Here is a cavalcade of animal life reminiscent of the monstrosities of Bosch's *Garden of Earthly Delights*: leeches, civets, blackbucks, roebucks, whitebaits, hammerheads, belugas, ferrets. One might also note the overt violence of their mode of life: drowning, fights, car accidents, injury, strangulation, and Stonewall Jackson (one of the more massacre-prone Civil War generals) thrown in for good measure. Gatsby, as a name, echoes the violence. One must recall that in the book Jay Gatsby is the hero's *assumed* name, not his real name. His real name is James Gatz. (His father, Henry Gatz, makes an appearance in the book's last few pages.) The significance of Gatsby and Gatz is in 'gat' – the gun which ends Gatsby's life. Violent death lingers around Gatsby. As the book opens he is just back from the war in Europe, which he is reputed to have quite enjoyed. Gatsby, it has also been pointed out, sounds, if you say it out loud, rather like the French verb *gaspiller*, to waste. Fitzgerald lived in France in the 1920s and wrote the book at Valescure, near St Raphael, so this is not impossible. Gatsby, by this reading, is thus one whose life is wasted in a violent encounter with a gat.

If 'Gatsby' is significant, so is 'Great'. In early drafts Fitzgerald had Gatsby refer to himself as 'great':

> 'Jay Gatsby!' he cried in a ringing voice, 'There goes the great Jay Gatsby! That's what people are going to say – wait and see. I'm only thirty-two now.'

But despite his legendary parties Gatsby is not 'great'. He is rootless, friendless, loveless and ultimately lifeless. Only three people come to his funeral. 'Great' is irony. Gatsby is a rich nobody.

Perhaps there is another echo in the 'great' of *The Great Gatsby*: that of 'the Great American Novel'. This was an artefact Fitzgerald was consciously trying to construct, after the pattern of Melville or James, and to which he paid homage in one of his final choices of title, *Under the Red, White and Blue*. Fitzgerald thought of *The Great Gatsby* as his greatest work; many of his readers have agreed. T.S. Eliot was among his admirers, and wrote to him in 1925 congratulating him on having significantly advanced the novel form with *Gatsby*.

The Great Gatsby, then, can be seen as Fitzgerald's attempt to represent his country in the medium of the novel. If this is so, then the title he finally chose is perfect, whatever his doubts. In the book, the dreams of greatness, wealth and success that form the nation's myth are brutally dispelled. In an atmosphere of high-class squalor Gatsby is meaninglessly shot down. In calling his book *The Great Gatsby* it seems that Fitzgerald was gunning for America.

34. WINNIE-THE-POOH
(1926)

How did Winnie-the-Pooh get his name? It is a question that
A.A. Milne was often asked – and came to dread. He came to
dread any mention of Pooh at all. If a review of his serious
books or plays – of which there were many – mentioned
Winnie-the-Pooh anywhere in its opening sentences, Milne
would know that the review was going to be a hostile one.

But at the risk of offending Milne's shade, it is rather a
good story.

The first strand came from the First World War. In 1914
Lieutenant Harry Colebourn was a twenty-seven-year-old
veterinary surgeon with the Canadian 34th Fort Garry Horse.
En route to Europe from his home town of Winnipeg, his
troop train stopped at White River, Ontario, where he saw a
hunter with a female black bear cub. The hunter had shot the
cub's mother, and Colebourn asked if he could buy it. A sale
was arranged for $20. Colebourn named the cub Winnipeg,
or Winnie, after his home town (he must have been home-
sick), and a few weeks later he and Winnie embarked with the
Canadian Army Veterinary Corps for England, the first stop
before the battlefields.

The cub became a popular mascot during the Corps's
initial encampment on Salisbury Plain, but in December 1914
it was decided that Flanders was not going to be a suitable
place for a bear, and Colebourn was ordered to find her alternative accommodation. On December 9, 1914 he entrusted
Winnie to the staff at London Zoo. He then left for the war.

Colebourn survived the fighting, intending all the time to
pick Winnie up on his way back from France, but in 1919 he
went home without her. The most likely reason is that Winnie,

who was very docile and sweet-natured, had become a prof-
itable attraction at the zoo. Another possible reason is that in
the war years she had grown into a huge adolescent bear.

The second strand came from a holiday the Milne family
took at Decoy Cottage, Poling, near Arundel, Sussex, some
time between 1921 and 1924. Milne's son Christopher Robin
(born in 1920 and so between one and four years old at the
time) was in the habit of feeding a swan on a nearby pond. As
Milne noted in the introduction to *When We Were Very
Young* (his first book for children, published in 1924):
'Christopher Robin, who feeds this swan in the mornings, has
given him the name of "Pooh". This is a very fine name for a
swan, because, if you call him and he doesn't come (which is a
thing swans are good at), then you can pretend that you were
just saying "Pooh!" to show how little you wanted him.' At
this point there is no suggestion that Pooh is anything else
other than a swan – although the volume does have a poem
about a bear called 'Teddy Bear', illustrated by E.H. Shepard
with a drawing that looks very much like Winnie-the-Pooh,
wearing his little armpit-high red jacket.

The third strand was to do with this very bear, Christopher Robin's favourite toy, whose name was then simply
Bear, Teddy Bear, or Edward Bear. Milne explains in the
introduction to *Winnie-the-Pooh*:

> Well, when Edward Bear said that he would like an
> exciting name all to himself, Christopher Robin said at
> once, without stopping to think, that he was Winnie-the-
> Pooh. And he was.

The reason was as follows:

> . . . when Christopher Robin goes to the Zoo, he goes to
> where the Polar Bears are, and he whispers something to

the third keeper from the left, and doors are unlocked, and we wander through dark passages and up steep stairs, until at last we come to the special cage, and the cage is opened, and out trots something brown and furry, and with a happy cry of 'Oh, Bear!' Christopher Robin rushes into its arms. Now this bear's name is Winnie, which shows what a good name for bears it is, but the funny thing is that we can't remember whether Winnie is called after Pooh, or Pooh after Winnie. We did know once, but we have forgotten . . .

It seems clear though that Pooh (the swan) could not have been named after Winnie (the bear), because otherwise in *When We Were Very Young* the swan would have been called Winnie. Perhaps that is applying adult logic to the situation. The crucial points of information are the dates of the respective communions with swan and bear. If the swan visit(s) predated the bear visit(s), then Edward Bear became associated with Pooh (the swan) and the final piece clicked into place after a subsequent meeting with Winnie the bear. If the bear visit(s) predated the swan visit(s), then Edward Bear became associated with Winnie (the bear), and the final piece clicked into place after a subsequent meeting with Pooh the swan. The first seems overwhelmingly more likely, and does seem to be the chronology by the evidence of the passages just quoted. It also seems unlikely that children who were little more than babies would have been allowed into bear cages, no matter how sweet and docile the natures of the bears inside. To add weight to the 'Pooh (the swan) first, Winnie (the bear) second' hypothesis there exists a photograph of Christopher Robin feeding Winnie with condensed milk at close quarters, showing a boy of about six.

Oddly enough, in the first chapter of the 1926 *Winnie-the-Pooh* there was a premonitory hint of the controversy around the book's title, as well as its author's disinclination to be pinned down on the subject. It was a disinclination that was characteristic of the tone of the book, and which perhaps later encouraged some to see *Winnie-the-Pooh* as a primer of existential gropings in general, or indeed of any or all philosophy:

> When I first heard his name, I said, just as you are going to say, 'But I thought he was a boy?'
>
> 'So did I,' said Christopher Robin.
>
> 'Then you can't call him Winnie?'
>
> 'I don't.'
>
> 'But you said –'
>
> 'He's Winnie-ther-Pooh. Don't you know what "ther" means?'
>
> 'Ah, yes, now I do,' I said quickly; and I hope you do too, because it is all the explanation you are going to get.

35. THE SUN ALSO RISES
(1926)

When Max Perkins,[1] Hemingway's editor at Scribner's, received the first draft of *The Sun Also Rises*, Hemingway's first major novel,[2] he was elated. He wrote back:

> *The Sun Also Rises* seems to me a most extraordinary performance. No one could conceive a book with more life in it. All the scenes, and particularly those when they cross the Pyrennees [sic] and come into Spain, and when they fish in that cold river, and when the bulls are sent in with the steers, and when they are fought in the arena, are of such a quality as to be like actual experience.

Not everyone agreed. Zelda Fitzgerald said later that it had three subjects: 'bullfighting, bullslinging and bullshitting'. Others criticized it for its wooden dialogue, ridiculous characters, overt anti-Semitism and misogyny. Max Perkins had a hard time convincing his chief, Charles Scribner, of its value. The story goes that Perkins jotted down on a pad some of the words that needed to be removed from Hemingway's manuscript: they included 'shit fuck bitch piss'. Unfortunately the heading on the pad was 'Things to do today'. Charles Scribner came into Perkins' office, saw the pad, and said to him: 'You must be exhausted.'[3]

The novel began its textual life in 1925 as a short story entitled 'Cayetano Ordonez' (the name of the bullfighter who provided the model for the fictional Pedro Romero). All the characters were based on Hemingway's friends, people with whom he had travelled in France and Spain: Brett Ashley was the real-life Lady Duff Twysden, Mike Campbell was Pat Guthrie,

Bill Gorton was Donald Ogden Stewart and Robert Cohn was Harold Loeb. In early drafts the main character (Jake Barnes) was even called 'Hem'. The relationships between the main characters – particularly Hem's (Jake's) unfulfilled love for Brett, Brett's affairs with Cohn, Mike and Romero, and Hem's antipathy to Cohn – were all closely modelled on life. 'I'm tearing those bastards apart,' Hemingway wrote to a friend in September 1925 as he was struggling with the book. 'I'm putting everyone in it and that kike Loeb is the villain.' And yet just after the title page Hemingway, the butter unmelted in his mouth, noted: 'No character in this book is the portrait of any actual person.'

As the story lengthened the title was changed to *Fiesta: A Novel* (which became its European title), and then, shortly before publication, *The Sun Also Rises*. Hemingway was a great user of quotations in titles, and *The Sun Also Rises* came from Ecclesiastes:

> What profit hath a man of all his labour which he taketh under the sun? One generation passeth away, and another generation cometh: but the earth abideth for ever. The sun also ariseth, and the sun goeth down, and hasteth to his place where he arose.

Hemingway gave the quotation in full as the epigraph to his book, counterposing it with an off-the-cuff remark from Gertrude Stein, which subsequently became as famous as (or more famous than) Ecclesiastes: 'You are all a lost generation.'[4] Hemingway meant to contrast the two quotes, containing as they both did the word 'generation', and later said that his purpose in so doing was to set the current generation of flawed humanity against the enduring power of the earth itself, the earth which 'abideth for ever'.

There is perhaps another nuance in *The Sun Also Rises*. It should be remembered that the central tragedy of the book is the genital wound of the hero, Jake Barnes. Jake, it has been pointed out by more than one commentator, rather closely parallels the Fisher King in T.S. Eliot's *The Waste Land*, published three years earlier in 1922 (see chapter 31). Jake's sexual incapacity is reflected in the decadent and morally sterile environment of Europe after the spiritual cataclysm of the First World War. Jake finds equilibrium only when he is fishing. Whether or not Eliot was a conscious influence, Jake's wound does symbolize the inability of any of the characters to find real meaning in their lives. It is because of Jake's wound – which Hemingway implies is a wound to his penis rather than just to his testicles – that Jake and Brett are unable to consummate their love for one another. Jake is instead forced into helping Brett seduce Romero. So if the book is closely autobiographical, and Jake is Hem, and Hem is Hemingway, where does that leave us?

On July 8, 1918, while serving as an ambulance driver on the Italian Front at the end of the First World War, Hemingway was seriously injured by a trench mortar, receiving over 200 separate shrapnel wounds to his lower body. His scrotum was pierced twice, and had to be laid on a special pillow while it recovered.[5] His testicles were undamaged and his penis intact. He had not lost his penis. But he knew a man who had:

> Because of this I got to know other kids who had genito urinary wounds and I wondered what a man's life would have been like after that if his penis had been lost and his testicles and spermatic cord remained intact. . . . [So I] tried to find out what his problems would be when he was in love with someone who was in love with him and there was nothing that they could do about it.

Jake has all the desires of a man but is never able to consummate them. The horror of such a wound represented the greatest of all horrors, and in *The Sun Also Rises* Hemingway was consciously confronting it. The fundamental act of masculinity, sexual penetration, is denied Jake, and the whole of the rest of masculinity which, for Hemingway, flowed from it – the bulls, the fights, the boxing, the hunting, the drinking, the bullshitting – is rendered pointless, a dreadful joke. It had so very nearly been a joke on Hemingway. He made the sexual connotations of the title clear in a letter to F. Scott Fitzgerald in late 1926, saying he was going to insert a subtitle in the next printing of the novel: 'The Sun Also Rises (Like Your Cock If You Have One).'

1 Max Perkins was also F. Scott Fitzgerald's editor: see chapter 33.

2 *The Torrents of Spring* (1926) is technically his first long fiction, but it was a youthful exercise in parody (of Sherwood Anderson): *The Sun Also Rises* was the beginning of the Hemingway style and his mature novelistic career.

3 There is more than one version of this story: in another version Scribner says: 'If you need reminding to do those things you're in a worse state than I thought.'

4 A more detailed account of the genesis of the remark can be found in *A Moveable Feast*, in which it is revealed that the phrase 'lost generation' was not a coining of Stein's, but that of an anonymous gas-station proprietor: 'It was when we had come back from Canada and were living in the rue Notre-Dame-des-Champs and Miss Stein and I were still good friends that Miss Stein made the remark about the lost generation. She had some ignition trouble with the old Model T Ford she then drove and the young man who worked in the garage and had served in the last year of the war had not been adept, or perhaps had not broken the priority of other vehicles, in repairing Miss Stein's Ford. Anyway he had not been *sérieux* and had been corrected severely by the patron of the garage after Miss Stein's protest. The patron had said to him, "You are all a *génération perdue*." "That's what you are. That's what you all are," Miss Stein said. "All of you young people who served in the war. You are a lost generation." "Really?" I said. "You are," she insisted. "You have no respect for anything . . ."'

5 The pillow is not available to view in the Hemingway Museum at Key West. Reports of the number of shrapnel wounds were confirmed by an American Red Cross representative, W.R. Castle, in a letter of July 20, 1918. Hemingway told Archibald MacLeish about the injuries to his scrotum in a letter of June 7, 1933.

36. THE ESCAPED COCK
(1928)

In early 1925, in Mexico, D.H. Lawrence contracted malaria. In his weakened state, tuberculosis took a hold, and for a few weeks he hovered between life and death. But in the spring of that year, on his ranch in New Mexico, he began to recover. Frieda wrote:

> How he loved every minute of life at the ranch. The morning, the squirrels, every flower that came in its turn, the big trees, chopping wood, the chickens, making bread, all our hard work, and the people all assumed the radiance of new life.

This personal resurrection was reflected in his writing. The period from 1925 to his death in 1930 was the period of *Lady Chatterley's Lover*, and the period too of *The Escaped Cock*, his last major work of fiction. One might say that in this last phase of his writing he was preoccupied by cocks. During these five years he also wrote the essays 'Women are so Cocksure', 'Cocksure Women and Hensure Men' and 'Aristocracy', the latter immediately after his illness in July 1925, in which he described his white cock Moses:

> And as the white cock calls in the doorway, who calls? Merely a barnyard rooster, worth a dollar-and-a-half. But listen! Under the old dawns of creation the Holy Ghost, the Mediator, shouts aloud in the twilight. And every time I hear him, a fountain of vitality gushes up in my body. It is life.

The cock is, with perfect Lawrentian seriousness, nature's phallus. And the bird is not some symbol from Frazer but the living embodiment of thrusting male energy, ready to fight and copulate at a moment's notice.

The novella *The Escaped Cock* was published in two parts, the first in 1928 and the second in 1929. It tells the story of Jesus' life immediately following his resurrection. In later years it was published as *The Man Who Died*, chiefly for reasons of prudery, but this was not the title preferred by Lawrence.

The plot, as Lawrence described it in a letter to a friend, is as follows:

> Jesus gets up and feels very sick about everything, and can't stand the old crowd any more – so cuts out – and as he heals up, he begins to find what an astonishing place the phenomenal world is, far more marvellous than any salvation or heaven – and thanks his stars he needn't have a 'mission' any more.

Jesus' first intimation that the phenomenal world is a marvellous place comes in the form of a barnyard cock escaping from a Galilean peasant:

> Advancing in a kind of half-consciousness under the drystone wall of the olive orchard, he was roused by the shrill, wild crowing of a cock just near him, a sound which made him shiver as if a snake had touched him [. . .] leaping out of the greenness, came the black-and-orange cock with the red comb, his tail-feathers streaming lustrous.

Jesus buys the cock from the peasant and goes on his way carrying it under his arm.

In the second part of the story we are introduced to a priestess of Isis. This woman has known both Caesar and Anthony, but has given herself to neither. She is a virgin, and waits for the man who can awaken her body. ('Rare women wait for the re-born man,' Lawrence comments – a good advertising slogan, if only one could think of the right product.) One morning she comes across Jesus lying asleep. 'For the first time, she was touched on the quick at the sight of a man [. . .] Men had aroused all sorts of feelings in her, but never had touched her on the yearning quick of her womb, with the flame tip of life.' The priestess and Jesus initiate one another into the life of the senses, a life which, until that moment, neither has known. Jesus sees the essential wrongness of his past ministry; he sees, suddenly, that saving souls has been, at bottom, a dry exercise:

> A vivid shame went through him. – After all, he thought, – I wanted them to love with dead bodies. If I had kissed Judas with live love, perhaps he would never have kissed me with death . . . There dawned on him the reality of the soft warm love which is in touch, and which is full of delight.

In the throes of this revelation, Jesus echoes the *Eli, Eli, lama sabachthani?* of the biblical Christ on the cross:

> He untied the string of the linen tunic, and slipped the garment down, till he saw the white glow of her white-gold breasts. And he touched them, and he felt his life go molten. – Father! He said – Why did you hide this from me? [. . .] Lo! He said. – This is beyond prayer.[1]

At the odd, evocative end of *The Escaped Cock*, a story that Lawrence might have continued had he lived, Jesus escapes by water, with the Romans in pursuit, presumably to recrucify him. Now, suddenly and differently fulfilled, he carries the priestess's perfume in his flesh 'like essence of roses'. The novella ends with the words: 'Tomorrow is another day.'

The title *The Escaped Cock* was suggested by something Lawrence noticed in Italy in 1927. At around this time he had developed a love of the culture of ancient Etruria (an interest that was later to have a flowering in the posthumous book *Etruscan Places*). After visiting the Etruscan tombs with his friend Earl Brewster, examining the frescoes with a battery torch, he wrote:

> The tombs seem so easy and friendly, cut out of rock underground. One does not feel oppressed, descending into them. It must be partly owing to the peculiar charm of natural proportion which is in all Etruscan things of the unspoilt, unromanticised centuries. There is a simplicity, combined with a most peculiar, free-breasted naturalness and spontaneity, in the shapes and move-ments of the underworld walls and spaces, that at once reassures the spirit. [. . .] And that is the true Etruscan quality: ease, naturalness, and an abundance of life, no need to force the mind or the soul in any direction.

After inspecting the tombs, Lawrence and Brewster were passing through the town of Volterra, and stopped for provisions. Brewster recalled what they saw:

> We passed a little shop, in the window of which was a toy rooster escaping from an egg. I remarked that it suggested the title – 'The Escaped Cock – a story of the Resurrection.' Lawrence replied that he had been think-ing about writing a story of the Resurrection.

Lawrence said in a letter to Harry Crosby that the model was of 'a cock escaping from a man', but he may have been confusing the model with the use he made of it in his story, in which the bird, tied by a string to a post, breaks free and runs off with the man pursuing it. But in both cases the cock was escaping. As Lawrence later wrote to Brewster about the title: 'It's called The Escaped Cock, from that toy in Volterra.'

It is all rather astonishing. If Lawrence and Brewster had not seen the toy, they would have had to have invented it. It brought together all of Lawrence's thinking: his fascination with the phallic cock-bird, his own sense of escape into a new life after his illness, and the story 'of the Resurrection' he had been considering, very probably one in which Jesus was imagined as a free-and-easy Etruscan, at home in his body, 'free-breasted' and spontaneous. At the centre of it all was a cosmic pun – Jesus as phallus, as the escaped cock himself. In this last fiction, here is the solemn, impressive, puritanically erotic Lawrence, with a double entendre that defies parody:

> The deep-folded, penetrable rock of the living woman! The woman, hiding her face. Himself bending over, powerful and new like dawn. He crouched to her, and he felt the blaze of his manhood and his power rise up in his loins, magnificent.
>
> 'I am risen!'

1 *The Escaped Cock* is written in a New Testament pastiche language which, as with much of Lawrence's writing, veers occasionally towards the ludicrous. 'So he came to an inn where asses stood in the yard. And he called for fritters, and they were made for him.'

37. MISS LONELYHEARTS
(1933)

Halfway through Nathanael West's harrowing novel of life in
1930s New York, the young hero confesses to his girlfriend
that he is posing as the female writer of an agony column:

> Perhaps I can make you understand. Let's start from the
> beginning. A man is hired to give advice to the readers of
> a newspaper. The job is a circulation stunt and the whole
> staff considers it a joke. He welcomes the job, for it
> might lead to a gossip column, and anyway he's tired of
> being a leg man. He too considers the job a joke, but
> after several months at it, the joke begins to escape him.
> He sees that the majority of the letters are profoundly
> humble pleas for moral and spiritual advice, that they are
> inarticulate expressions of genuine suffering. He also
> discovers that his correspondents take him seriously. For
> the first time in his life, he is forced to examine the values
> by which he lives. This examination shows him that he is
> the victim of the joke and not its perpetrator.

The young man's new-found knowledge does not lead to
any redemption, but to a slowly gathering insanity. Tormented by the pathos of the letters, the cynicism of Shrike, his
editor,[1] the unspeakable scenes of daily life in Depression
America ('He saw a man who appeared to be on the verge of
death stagger into a movie theater that was showing a picture
called *Blonde Beauty*. He saw a ragged woman with an
enormous goiter pick a love story magazine out of a garbage
can and seem very excited by her find'), Miss Lonelyhearts –
for that is the young man's byline, and the only title he is ever

given in the book – winds to his drunken, sticky, bloody end. It was West's second novel[2] and was critically very well received, although, for reasons connected with a legal dispute, it had very poor sales.

The pivotal moment in the creation of *Miss Lonelyhearts* occurred in 1929, while West was working as an assistant manager at the Kenmore Hall Hotel on East 23rd Street, New York. One night in March, West's friend the satirist S.J. Perelman dropped by and asked West if he would care to come along to Siegel's, a restaurant in Greenwich Village, where he was going to meet a friend who wrote an agony column for the *Brooklyn Eagle* under the name of Susan Chester. 'Susan' had said that she had some readers' letters that Perelman might be able to use as comic material. West agreed, and they all read the letters over dinner. It soon became clear that the letters were not really suitable for Perelman: they were full of tragic tales of unwanted pregnancies, hopeless love, tubercular husbands and dead children, and were signed with pseudonyms such as 'Despairing', 'Down-hearted wife' or 'Broad Shoulders'. But they were a revelation to West. Deeply moved by the simplicity of the appeals for help, he took the bundle of letters back to the hotel with him and for the next few weeks studied them. He read them aloud to friends, who reported that, uncharacteristically, he seemed to be experiencing strong empathy with these toilers: he was, one reported, 'terribly . . . hurt by them'.

At the same time West received a promotion. In 1930 he moved from the Kenmore Hall Hotel to the position of full manager at the Sutton Club Hotel on East 56th Street. His friends now referred to him as 'P.N. West, the great writer and bordello-keeper' (the 'P' was for 'Pep', West's nickname). In his capacity as manager he was free to allocate any of the empty rooms gratis to friends, many of whom happened to be struggling writers. As time went by the Sutton was occupied by, among others, the Perelmans, Edmund Wilson, Lillian Hellman, James T. Farrell, Dashiell Hammett and Erskine Caldwell. The hotel underwent a transformation into a nexus of 1930s literary talent. West's position as manager meant that he had full control of the hotel's mail, and he and Lillian Hellman began to entertain themselves by steaming open the letters of the guests. They found that the clientele led lives richer in *grotesquerie* and self-destructiveness even than the correspondents of the *Brooklyn Eagle*. Ex-movie extras were selling themselves to any takers, male or female; suicides were planned and executed, one person leaping from the hotel terrace through the glass ceiling of the dining room while dinner was in progress.

The two influences fused. West took the 'Susan Chester' lonely hearts letters and combined them with his secret knowledge of the inhabitants of the Sutton, and between 1930 and 1932 produced *Miss Lonelyhearts*. It is generally considered his finest work. *Miss Lonelyhearts* went beyond the practised cynicism of Dorothy Parker, Perelman and West's other literary friends of the 1930s into an area of quite terrifying human degradation.

It is interesting to think that it would never have happened had it not been for the rather pernicious habit of reading other people's letters.

1 Shrike and Miss Lonelyhearts very probably provided the idea for the Guru Brahmin in Evelyn Waugh's *The Loved One* (1948).
2 His first was *The Dream Life of Balso Snell* (1931) and his only other major novel *The Day of the Locust* (1939).

38. THE POSTMAN
ALWAYS RINGS TWICE
(1934)

James M. Cain was the writer responsible for some of the classic 'tough-guy' novels of the 1930s and 1940s: *The Postman Always Rings Twice*, *Double Indemnity*, *Mildred Pierce*, *Serenade*, *The Embezzler* and others. Many of these were made into films: *The Postman Always Rings Twice* was filmed in 1946 and 1981, with a French version in 1939 and an Italian version (Visconti's *Ossessione*) in 1942.

The tough-guy novel was distinct from the hard-boiled private-detective novel of Chandler or Hammett. It dealt less with the solving of crimes than with the aimless lives of the drifters and hustlers of the Depression, and was characterized by fast-paced action, seedy backdrops, laconic dialogue and plenty of violence and sex. On the opening page of *The Postman* we meet Frank Chambers, a bum, being thrown off a hay truck outside a roadside inn. Soon he is running his eye over Cora Papadakis, the wife of the inn's proprietor:

> Then I saw her. She had been out back, in the kitchen, but she came in to gather up the dishes. Except for the shape, she really wasn't any raving beauty, but she had a sulky look to her, and her lips stuck out in a way that made me want to mash them in for her.

A few pages later Frank takes matters in hand:

> She started for the lunchroom again, but I stopped her. 'Let's – leave it locked.'

'Nobody can get in if it's locked. I got some cooking to do. I'll wash up this plate.'

I took her in my arms and mashed my mouth up against hers . . . 'Bite me! Bite me!'

I bit her. I sunk my teeth into her lips so deep I could feel the blood spurt into my mouth. It was running down her neck when I carried her upstairs.

The lovers perceive that the murder of the husband will help things along, and accomplish it around page 45. They are immediately arrested. Once in custody they betray one another, but are released after some shady dealings with their defence attorney. They try to rebuild their lives, but Cora dies in a car accident. Frank is arrested for her murder, and writes the last sentence of the book just as he is about to be hanged.

The book's title was originally *Bar-B-Q* (there is a sign offering Bar-B-Q outside the inn) but Cain's publisher, Alfred Knopf, disliked it and asked for a change. Cain came up with *The Postman Always Rings Twice*, which Knopf disliked even more, but Cain would not be budged a second time. According to Cain the title came about as a result of a conversation with a screenwriter, Vincent Lawrence.

Lawrence was, by all accounts, an eccentric figure. Cain, who was also making a poor living as a screenwriter at the time, described him in the preface to *Three of a Kind*: 'He had fantastic names for his friends, and spoke a fantastic language of his own, with words in it I am not sure, well as I have come to know him, I really understand, at least in their relation to his cerebration.' Lawrence plotted out his screenplays around a device he called a 'love-rack', which Cain interpreted as a device whereby the characters are tormented by obsessive desires which drive the plot. Cain described how one day Lawrence was telling him how nervous he had been after mailing off his first play to a producer:

Then, he said, 'I almost went nuts. I'd sit and watch for the postman, and then I'd think, "You got to cut this out," and then when I left the window I'd be listening for his ring. How I'd know it was the postman was that he'd always ring twice.'

He went on with more of the harrowing tale, but I cut in on him suddenly. I said: 'Vincent, I think you've given me a title for that book.'

'What's that?'

'The Postman Always Rings Twice.'

'Say, he rang twice for Chambers, didn't he?'

'That's the idea.'

'And on that second ring, Chambers had to answer, didn't he? Couldn't hide out in the backyard any more.'

'His number was up, I'd say.'

'I like it.'

'Then that's it.'

This would be the end of the story behind *The Postman Always Rings Twice* were it not for the fact that there is no postman in the book, no doorbell, and no single, dual, or any ring. Frank Chambers does not 'hide out in the backyard', nor does he 'have to answer'. Neither is there any prior version of the book in which any of these things occur.

Cain, it seems, was speaking metaphorically. The book is structured around two main events: the murder of the husband and the death of the wife. Chambers had a hand in both of them, but after the second death, 'his number was up', 'he couldn't hide'. He had played deaf to the first ring, but was forced to respond to the second. The 'postman' was fate, nemesis, retribution, divine justice; and the parcel that awaited Frank was the recorded delivery of his own demise. The postman, after all, *always* rings twice. Justice will be done: the Aristotelian formula is preserved. The ineluctable

course of cause and effect brings about the ultimate consequences of the deed, *katastrophein*, or the overturning, ruin,
or *bouleversement* of all earthly plans.

The ready way that Lawrence understood Cain's meaning
is believable, given that they were both exponents of a craft in
which there is a preoccupation with what lies *behind* events:
three-act structure, reversals and re-reversals, pay-offs and
love-racks. Or perhaps it is not so believable. Wouldn't 'What
the hell are you talking about?' have been a more likely
response from Lawrence? In the final analysis we only have
Cain to go on, and the line of least resistance is to trust him.

The Postman was a huge bestseller, and Cain became rich
and famous. The title was a major contributor to the book's
success. The image of the postman is a particularly good one.
The postman is a lone male,[1] not unlike his co-worker the
iceman – or like Frank Chambers. Lone males calling on
houses during the daytime may encounter lone females. What
are the two rings but a secret signal? What is on the end of a
secret signal but love? The title is suggestive but enigmatic,
domestic but menacing, gnomic but nonsensical. It is hard to
believe that *The Postman Always Rings Twice* would have
been filmed with Lana Turner and John Garfield, and later
with Jessica Lange and Jack Nicholson, had it been called
Bar-B-Q.

[1] One thinks of the sexually predatory postman-protagonist of Charles
Bukowski's *Post Office*.

39. NO THANKS

(1935)

In the summer of 1934 the normally buoyant E.E. Cummings[1] was in low water. His ballet *Tom*, based on *Uncle Tom's Cabin* by Harriet Beecher Stowe, had been pronounced undanceable by George Balanchine, and had been dropped by the American Ballet. A Hollywood screenwriting offer worth around $10,000 had been made in August but then inexplicably withdrawn. He had been awarded a Guggenheim Fellowship worth $1,500, but the money had run out. More brutally, the poems he had written with the Guggenheim money had proved unpublishable. Tentatively entitled *70 Poems*, the volume had been turned down by fourteen publishers.

The Depression was taking a toll on American publishers and American readers. Poetry, never anything less than a luxury, was selling very badly, and Cummings' brand of experimental verse was doing worse than most. In the 1920s he had found publishers for his poetry because of his one indisputable hit, the novel *The Enormous Room*. But his poetry had never sold well. In the first half of 1935 Cummings' publishers Liveright sold 13 copies of *Is 5* and just two copies of *ViVa*, and Covici-Friede managed to push exactly one copy of *Eimi*.

In the face of this *70 Poems* was a magnificent refusal to compromise. It was a highly wrought, precisely structured collection, organized into a schema which alternated sonnets with free verse poems, representing the descent from heaven to earth and back to heaven. The structure as Cummings conceived it (though this was not published with the volume) was as follows:

2 'moon' poems	2 'star' poems[2]
sonnet I	sonnet XVIII
3 poems	3 poems
sonnet II	sonnet XVII
3 poems	3 poems
sonnet III	sonnet XVI
3 poems	3 poems
sonnet IV	sonnet XV
3 poems	3 poems
sonnet V	sonnet XIV
3 poems	3 poems
sonnet VI	sonnet XIII
3 poems	3 poems
sonnet VII	sonnet XII
3 poems	3 poems
sonnet VIII	sonnet XI
3 poems	3 poems

'earth' sonnet IX   'earth' sonnet X

1 poem

Thematically the volume focused on the natural world, the doings within the miniature cosmoi of grasshoppers, ants and mice, the joy of spring awakenings, the sun's and moon's rises and settings, and love between man and woman. Form was central: in poem thirteen, for example, there is an exhilarating typographical attempt to suggest a grasshopper's leap and self-rearrangement; and in poem nine there is an attempt to conjure the effect of the announcement, through echoing loudspeakers at a baseball game, of 'The President of the United States', the lengthening lines and increasing capitalization forming a wedge-shaped crescendo:

> (The president The
> president of The president
> of the The)president of
>
> the(united The president of the
> united states The president of the united
> states of The President Of The)United States

After his fourteen failures Cummings gave up and turned to his mother. She gave him $300, with which he approached the printer Samuel Jacobs to bring out the volume under his own imprint, the Golden Eagle Press. The title was changed from *70 Poems* to *No Thanks*, in allusion to the publishers' polite refusals. To put the final nail in the coffin Cummings included on the book's dedication page a concrete poem, arranging the fourteen publishers in the form of a funeral urn:

NO

THANKS

TO

Farrar & Rinehart

Simon & Schuster

Coward-McCann

Limited Editions

Harcourt, Brace

Random House

Equinox Press

Smith & Haas

Viking Press

Knopf

Dutton

Harper's

Scribner's

Covici-Friede

1 E.E. Cummings preferred to capitalize the initials of his name in his correspondence, on book jackets and in other material. See Norman Friedman, 'Not "e. e. cummings" Revisited', (1996).
2 Cummings' own schema in the 1978 Liveright edition, slightly adapted.

40. NINETEEN EIGHTY-FOUR
(1949)

The early 1980s were not the most cheerful of times. Two heavily armed power blocs were keeping the world in a state of perpetual phoney war. There were authoritarian governments and repressive police forces. The western world was looking forward to a date signalling the obliteration of all hope and human values. The countdown to 1984 was more 'millennial' than the real millennium sixteen years later. The only people who really seemed to be enjoying it were advertising copywriters:

> WAR IS PEACE. FREEDOM IS SLAVERY. IGNORANCE IS STRENGTH. And our new crisp Sisal-like look in wool broadloom is $19.84 a sq. yd. (padding and installation not included). At $19.84 it's well worth watching, Big Brother.[1]

On New Year's Day 1984 we seemed to have entered, not a year, but a ghastly stage set. For forty years George Orwell had been treated as a latter-day Nostradamus. Now, here at last, was the year in which Orwell would be proved right or wrong.

Attempts were made from the moment of its publication to find significance in the date of *Nineteen Eighty-Four*. The best-known explanation was the 'year-reversal' theory. Orwell finished the book in December 1948, and '48' reversed is '84'. But when Orwell began writing the book, in 1943, the action was set in 1980. As time wore on he advanced the date to 1982, and then to 1984. He may well have been aware of the year-reversal as he completed the manuscript, but fundamentally the date of

1984 was a product of the fact that he had taken such a long time to write the book.

The next best-known theory is the 'Jack London' argument. In London's dystopia *The Iron Heel* (1908), a book Orwell admired greatly, the USA is run along fascist lines by a group of Oligarchs who control the population via the Mercenaries.[2] In the story, the date of the completion of the 'wonder-city' Asgard is – 1984. But 1984 is not a particularly prominent date in London's book. In fact it appears in a footnote describing the construction of two cities: 'Ardis was completed in A.D.1942, while Asgard was not completed until A.D.1984. It was fifty-two years in the building, during which time a permanent army of half a million serfs was employed.' If it had been Orwell's intention to allude to *The Iron Heel*, one might have expected to find the date 1984 earlier in manuscript versions of *Nineteen Eighty-Four*.

An intriguing third argument concentrates on a poem by Orwell's first wife, Eileen O'Shaughnessy, published in a school magazine in 1934. It is called 'End of the Century: 1984', and deals with a future society in which 'scholars' are controlled by telepathy: they 'tune their thought/to Telepathic Station 9/From which they know just what they ought'. Orwell could have been thinking of this in 1948 when he came to name the book, but it does not seem very likely: again, it would probably have appeared much earlier in the manuscripts.

Nineteen eighty-four, it seems clear, was not a date of particular significance for Orwell. A couple of facts clinch the matter. The first is that Orwell's working title for the book was *The Last Man in Europe*.[3] Even after its completion in late 1948, Orwell was still discussing the title with his publisher, Frederic Warburg, and writing to a friend: 'I haven't definitely fixed on the title but I am hesitating between NINETEEN EIGHTY-FOUR and THE LAST MAN

IN EUROPE.' The second is that Orwell's US publishers, Harcourt Brace, had expressed doubts about the title *Nineteen Eighty-Four*, and asked Orwell for permission to retitle it.[4] Orwell wrote to his agent: 'I doubt whether it hurts a book to be published under different names in Britain and the USA – certainly it is often done – and I would like Harcourt Brace to follow their own wishes in the matter of the title.' If *Nineteen Eighty-Four* had been intended as a homage to his dead wife, or as a coded reference to *The Iron Heel*, or as a piece of numerology, would he not have been more concerned?

Rarely can a date chosen with such little particularity have exercised such a frightful grip on the imagination. A collective sigh of relief was exhaled as December 31, 1984 slipped away and 1985 began (despite the fact that Anthony Burgess had written a rather indifferent book about it). The date that was, more than any other, symbolic of 'the future' was now past. *Nineteen Eighty-Four* was a failed future, and had suffered the common fate of all prophecies from St John the Divine to Mother Shipton. George Orwell was now revealed in his true colours. He was The Man Who Had Got It Wrong. Never mind that he had repeatedly said that his book was not a prophecy and that it should instead be considered a 'satire'.[5] He had cast a shadow over us for four decades, staring from old photographs and book jackets with his pencil moustache and his silly haircut. We had put up with his prediction of a new Dark Age, and now *Nineteen Eighty-Four* could be consigned to the memory hole.

Among advertising copywriters there was once again a spurt of interest, this time pointing out how the human spirit, with a little help from capitalism and the free market, had triumphed. The Olivetti Computer Company was among those stamping on Orwell, with a full-page advertisement featuring a chubby girl cuddling a lamb:

1984; ORWELL WAS WRONG. According to Orwell, in 1984 man and computer would become enemies. But his pessimistic outlook was wrong. Today, the computers produced by the world's leading companies are man's most reliable aid. And the Olivetti M20 personal computer proves it.

1 Print advertisement for the Einstein Moomjy Carpet Company in New York, early 1984.

2 A situation strongly reminiscent of the ideal state in Plato's *Republic* (see chapter 1), a work which Orwell also echoed in the tripartite division of society into Inner Party, Outer Party and Proles.

3 At one point O'Brien says to Winston: 'If you are a man, Winston, you are the last man. Your kind is extinct; we are the inheritors.'

4 In the event, of course, they did not.

5 Orwell wrote in more than one press release in 1949 that the book was a satire. But a satire of what? Several targets have been suggested. One of the most likely is a work by the American political theorist James Burnham, who in 1940 had written a book entitled *The Managerial Revolution*. In this book Burnham speculated that the heirs to the world's great capitalist, communist and fascist power blocs would be a new breed of political 'managers' – that is, unelected oligarchs whose only *raison d'être* would be to stay in power. In an essay of 1946 Orwell argued against this idea: 'Fortunately the "managers" are not so invincible as Burnham believes. The huge, invincible, everlasting slave empire of which Burnham appears to dream will not be established.'

41. THE LION, THE WITCH AND THE WARDROBE
(1950)

There are very few books with the formula 'The x, the x and the x'. 'The x and the x' is very common: *The Ring and the Book*; *The Oak and the Calf*; *The Naked and the Dead*; *The Sound and the Fury* – the list could go on. The only genre in which one finds a profusion of titles of the three-barrelled variety is in fairy tales. Thus we have *The Knapsack, The Hat and The Horn*; *The Mouse, the Bird and the Sausage*; *One-Eye, Two-Eyes and Three-Eyes*; *The Spindle, The Shuttle and The Needle*; *The Straw, the Coal and the Bean*. C.S. Lewis's *The Lion, the Witch and the Wardrobe* was intended to fit into the fairy-tale tradition.[1]

In his book of essays *Of Other Worlds* Lewis said that it all began with mental images:

> All my seven Narnia books, and my three science fiction books, began with seeing pictures in my head. At first they were not a story, just pictures. The *Lion* all began with a picture of a faun carrying an umbrella and parcels in a snowy wood. This picture had been in my mind since I was about sixteen. Then one day, when I was about forty, I said to myself: 'Let's try to make a story about it.' At first I had very little idea how the story would go. But then suddenly Aslan[2] came bounding into it. I think I had been having a good many dreams of lions about that time. Apart from that, I don't know where the Lion came from or why He came. But once He was there, He pulled the whole story together, and soon He pulled the six other Narnian stories in after Him.

When it came to the witch, the influences went beyond mental pictures. In 1948 Lewis remarked to a friend, Chad Walsh, that he was attempting a children's book 'in the tradition of E. Nesbit'. Nesbit is in fact central to understanding not only the first Narnia book but the whole of the series. Nesbit wrote about dragons, magic, ancient Egypt, travel in time and space, socialism and wishes coming true; perhaps more importantly for Lewis's fiction she wrote about extraordinary things happening to ordinary children. Lewis read most of her tales as a child, and when setting *The Magician's Nephew* in the not-so-distant past, wrote: 'In those days Mr Sherlock Holmes was still living in Baker Street and the Bastables [Nesbit's sextet of heroes] were looking for treasure in the Lewisham Road . . .' In one Nesbit adventure, *The Story of the Amulet*, we find the prototype for Jadis, the White Witch, in the person of the Queen of Babylon. Like Jadis, the Queen is haughty, magnificently dressed, physically imposing and liable to shout things such as 'Kill the dogs!' She is summoned to London by magic, as is Jadis in *The Magician's Nephew*, and once there she creates a very similar style of havoc. In *The Story of the Amulet* there is even an 'Uncle Andrew' figure in the person of a 'learned gentleman' who lives upstairs.

There are numerous other Nesbit echoes throughout the Narnia series. One deserves special consideration: the detail of the wardrobe.

In 1908 Nesbit published a story in *Blackie's Christmas Annual* called 'The Aunt and Amabel'. Eight-year-old Amabel has displeased her aunt by cutting the heads off all the flowers in the greenhouse, and has been sent to the 'best bedroom' as a punishment. While incarcerated she begins looking through a book of railway timetables, and discovers a destination called 'Whereyouwanttogoto':

This was odd – but the name of the station from which it started was still more extraordinary, for it was not Euston or Cannon Street or Marylebone.

The name of the station was 'Bigwardrobeinspareroom.' And below this name, really quite unusual for a station, Amabel read in small letters:

'Single fares strictly forbidden. Return tickets No Class Nuppence. Trains leave Bigwardrobeinspareroom all the time.'

And under that in still smaller letters –

'You had better go now.'

What would you have done? Rubbed your eyes and thought you were dreaming? Well, if you had, nothing more would have happened. Nothing ever does when you behave like that. Amabel was wiser. She went straight to the Big Wardrobe and turned its glass handle.

Amabel goes through the wardrobe and finds a curious railway station, whence she is launched into a little adventure.[3] Lucy goes through the wardrobe in the spare room and encounters Mr Tumnus, the faun:

'I – I got in through the wardrobe in the spare room,' said Lucy.

'Ah! If only I had worked harder at geography when I was a little Faun,' said Mr. Tumnus, 'I'd know all about strange countries.'

'The wardrobe is not a country. It's only back there where it's summer,' said Lucy.

'It has been winter for so long in Narnia,' said the Faun sadly. 'Daughter of Eve from the far land of Spare Oom, would you have tea with me?'

It is not Nesbit's best story – Amabel wakes up and finds it is all a dream – but the resemblances are interesting.

Of course *The Lion, the Witch and the Wardrobe* is not simply a product of Lewis's reworkings of Nesbit, Edmund Spenser, Milton, Hans Christian Andersen, Lewis Carroll, George Macdonald, or anyone else. Even if one were to tally up all the echoes of Lewis's vast reading in *The Lion*, the whole is a fully imagined and 'believable' telling of what four children do when they go through a wardrobe into a snowy wood, and what happens when the snow begins to melt.

But one source does have a truly structural influence on the book, one which it would be foolish to skate over: the New Testament. The Lion of the title ('Him') is a stand-in for another personage entirely. Lewis was rather resistant to the idea that his book was merely a Christian allegory. He wrote in *Of Other Worlds*:

> Some people seem to think that I began by asking myself how I could say something about Christianity to children; then fixed on the fairy tale as an instrument; then collected information about child-psychology and decided what age group I'd write for; then drew up a list of basic Christian truths and hammered out 'allegories' to embody them. This is all pure moonshine.

Is this back-pedalling? In June 1953 Lewis received a question from a young reader. She wanted to know what Aslan had meant when he said to Lucy in *The Dawn Treader* that in her world he was known by 'another name'. Lewis replied:

> As to Aslan's other name, well I want you to guess. Has there never been anyone in *this* world who (1.) Arrived at the same time as Father Christmas. (2.) Said he was the

son of the Great Emperor. (3.) Gave himself up for someone else's fault to be jeered at and killed by wicked people. (4.) Came to life again. (5.) Is sometimes spoken of as a Lamb (see the end of the Dawn Treader). Don't you really know His name in this world. Think it over and let me know your answer!

1 Three is of course a magical number in fairy tales, and in the titles of fairy tales: *The Three Spinners*, *The Three Snake-Leaves* and *The Three Feathers* are three examples. One might also note that Lewis plays slightly on the 'three' motif by employing a deliberate note of bathos: after a lion and a witch (two plausible fairy-tale characters) a wardrobe seems slightly silly.

2 The name Aslan is Turkish for lion. It is only one of a number of Turkish references in the series. The witch's name is Jadis, and the Turkish for witch is *cadı* (The '*c*' is pronounced with a 'j' sound, and the vowel at the end has a sound similar to 'uh'). Edmund is of course offered Turkish delight. The Calormenes are distinctly Turkic.

3 Railway stations as a node for magical travel between worlds are also featured in the Narnia stories.

42. WAITING FOR GODOT
(1952)

In the matter of titles, brute power of coincidence is likely to throw up strange shapes. Did Vladimir Nabokov read von Lichberg's 'Lolita' (see chapter 43)? Did George Orwell remember the footnote in chapter 21 of Jack London's *The Iron Heel* (see chapter 40)? No diaries or notes give any clue, and we are forced to sift possibilities, aware that certainty will probably always be unobtainable. But it is when we begin to see multiple influences, all equally compelling, probable, and mutually contradictory, that we begin to despair. And the title that invites the greatest despair of all is *Waiting for Godot*.

Godot was written in French, in Paris, in 1948/9, and was published in 1952. It was first performed in English at the Arts Theatre, London, in 1955. The critic Vivian Mercier wrote a famous review for the *Irish Times* in 1956 which said that it was a play 'in which nothing happens, twice.' It was at first greeted with incomprehension and distaste,[1] but by the late 1950s was recognized by critics such as Kenneth Tynan as a landmark in world theatre. It was not long before attention was focusing on one word: 'Godot'. What did it mean?

The question naturally, was put to Beckett himself. He gave several replies. The most frequent was that it came from *godillot*, a type of clumsy boot. Boots are prominent in the play: Estragon is always taking off and pulling on his boots. To another questioner he replied: 'there is a rue Godot, a cycling racer named Godot . . .' Beckett seemed positively to wish that the name should be woven from several strands at once. Other interpreters conspired in bringing this state of affairs about.

There are theories that Godot comes from a Gaelic dialect word meaning 'forever'. That it is an amalgam of the nick-names of the two main characters (Didi + Gogo = Godot). That the title derives from a work of 1950 by Simone Weil, *Attente de Dieu* ('Waiting for God'). That it derives from an incident in which Beckett met a group of bicyclists and asked them 'What are you waiting for?' and the reply came 'We are waiting for Godot.' That Godot is God. That the *-ot* suffix makes a diminutive of God, on the pattern of Pierre/Pierrot. That it is intended to echo Charlot, the French name for Charlie Chaplin (the characters all wear bowler hats). That it evokes French words beginning with *god-* which have vulgar meanings: *godemiché*, dildo; *godelureau*, fop; *godiche*, oafish; *à la godille*, ropy; *godailleur,* guzzler.

One could wait around for a lifetime for the right answer. But one possibility, first explored by Eric Bentley in his *What is Theatre?* (1956), is particularly interesting. This is that Beckett took the name from a character in an obscure play by Balzac called *Le Faiseur* (in other editions, *Mercadet*). The play revolves around a stock-market trader, Mercadet, who is going bankrupt. His funds are all tied up with his ex-partner, Godeau, who is mysteriously elusive. Mercadet makes it clear to his creditors that once Godeau arrives, everyone will get paid. Until then, all they can do is wait. By the end of the play disaster seems imminent, but then the arrival of Godeau is announced. He had just come back from India where he has made a huge fortune. Everyone is going to get paid. The rapturous Mercadet exclaims, 'Let's go and see Godeau!' It is the last line of the play. In the last line of *Waiting for Godot* Estragon also says 'Yes, let's go.' The stage direction then grimly reads, 'They do not move.'

Could Beckett have read this obscure play, been impressed by the idea of a character who exists only offstage, whose existence is vital to the characters and yet can never be pinned down, whose intervention is devoutly desired but who never materializes, and is called Godeau? It is certainly possible. One could take it a step further and say that Beckett need not have read the play. He could have gone to the Comédie Française, who put the play on in 1935–6, while he was living in Paris. Or to the Tournées Charles Baret, who put it on in 1936–7. Or to the Théâtre de l'Atelier in 1940 or the Théâtre Sarah Bernhardt in 1945. Beckett need not even have gone to the theatre. He could have seen it at the cinema. In 1936 a film of *Le Faiseur* was released in France. Perhaps most interestingly of all, it was adapted as an English-language film in 1949, the year *Waiting for Godot* was being written, starring Buster Keaton, one of Beckett's favourite actors. The title of this film was *The Lovable Cheat*, and starred Charles Ruggles as Mercadet and Keaton as Goulard (a creditor of Mercadet).

It is rather satisfying to think that this keystone of theatrical modernism could have had its origin at the pictures.

1 The Lord Chamberlain objected to the word 'erection' and demanded it be docked. A letter from Lady Dorothy Howitt to the Lord Chamberlain asked for the play to be banned outright, and gave in evidence that 'One of the many themes running through the play is the desire of two old tramps continually to relieve themselves. Such a dramatization of lavatory necessities is offensive and against all sense of British decency.'

43. LOLITA
(1955)

Did she have a precursor? She did, indeed she did. In point of fact, there might have been no Lolita at all had I not loved, one summer, a certain initial girl-child.

Lolita

Lolita is one of those novels in which the protagonist-narrator is so coruscatingly brilliant that we are ready to forgive him almost anything. Twelve-year-olds? Well, she *did* seduce him. And she'd already had that boy at summer camp. And sex with young girls would be regarded as quite normal in many cultures. For prose this dazzling, this ardent, this clever . . . *tout comprendre c'est tout pardonner* . . .

But plagiarism?

This is the most recent charge against Nabokov's notorious book, explored notably in Michael Maar's *The Two Lolitas*, a volume to which this chapter is largely indebted. The facts are these. In 1916 a German journalist, Heinz von Eschwege, writing under the name of Heinz von Lichberg, published a collection of stories called *The Accursed Gioconda*. Buried about halfway through the collection was a little story – only twelve pages long – called 'Lolita'. It is a ghost story in a sub-Poe vein, perhaps with a dash of Thomas Mann thrown in. The narrator, a student living in southern Germany, makes the acquaintance of a pair of brothers, two old men who run a tavern. The impression they produce on him is one of 'something unspeakably weary, fearful, and all but tragic'. One night he overhears a violent altercation between the brothers as he is passing the tavern; he does not dare go in, but the next morning they seem quite normal. The student then departs for

Alicante in Spain, where he stays at a hotel and meets the daughter of the household, Lolita, a young girl (he does not say *how* young, but 'by our northern standards she was terribly young'), and is smitten by an unholy lust. One night his dirty young man's dreams come true:

> Lolita sat on my balcony and sang softly, as she often did. But this time she came to me with halting steps on the landing, the guitar discarded precipitously onto the floor. And while her eyes sought out the image of the flickering moon in the water, like a pleading child she flung her trembling little arms around my neck, leaned her head on my chest, and began sobbing. There were tears in her eyes, but her sweet mouth was laughing. The miracle had happened. 'You are so strong,' she whispered.
>
> Days and nights came and went; the mystery of beauty held them entwined in an unchangeable, singing serenity.

After a few weeks of passion (no details are given) the student has a terrible vision, in which he sees the two brothers from the tavern arguing fiercely over Lolita, and then strangling her. Reeling from the experience, he discovers that Lolita has died in the night. Lolita's father, who takes the news quite phlegmatically, reveals to the student that her death is the result of a family curse. Lolita's mother, grand-mother, great-grandmother, great-great-grandmother and great-great-great-grandmother were all murdered as young women shortly after giving birth to a girl-child, who was then murdered in turn a few short years later, also after giving birth to a girl-child. Lolita, who has not given birth, is the end of the line. The student leaves the *pension*, returns to Germany and finds that the brothers (the original seducers of the great-great-great-grandmother, we assume) have also been found dead, 'with a friendly smile on their faces'.

The story is short, silly and uninvolving. The book as a whole did not sell particularly well. But the similarities with Nabokov's *Lolita* seem too many to discount. In Nabokov's novel, the narrator, Humbert Humbert, who recounts his 'Confession of a White Widowed Male' while in prison for murder, tells how, having recently arrived in the USA from France, he stays at a small boarding house in a small town and is smitten with unholy lust for the landlady's twelve-year-old daughter, Lolita. He marries Lolita's mother, Charlotte Haze, who dies conveniently in a car accident leaving him free to 'look after' Lolita. Finally Lolita dies (a few weeks after giving birth, though not to his child) and he kills her lover, Quilty.

The main similarities of plot and construction, then, are these: both have a first-person narrator who turns up at a boarding house; Lolita in both cases is the daughter of the house; she 'seduces' him; sex and death (and death after birth) are presented as different aspects of the same violence, or as cause and effect; and finally the book/story's title is 'Lolita'.

Of course, Nabokov would probably not have read those twelve pages in an obscure, untranslated book by a minor German writer, published when he (Nabokov) was seventeen and still living in Russia. Or would he? Nabokov left Russia with his family in 1919, and after three years studying at Cambridge, settled in Berlin in 1922. He remained there for fifteen years – until 1937 – married there, had a son, wrote several novels, and made his pre-*Lolita* reputation. These were fifteen years in which von Lichberg was a fellow Berliner, even living in the same part of Berlin. The book was still in the shops, and Nabokov read German quite adequately. Lichberg, meanwhile, was becoming quite prominent as a public figure. He was one of the commentators in a well-known German newsreel of 1933, on the occasion of the torchlight parade celebrating Hitler's accession to the Reichs-Chancellorship. After serving in the military police of the Abwehr in Poland during the Second World War, von Lichberg retired with the rank of lieutenant-colonel, and died in 1951.

What can we make of the similarities between the two stories? Four possibilities suggest themselves. The first is coincidence, but given the sheer number of matches, this seems the least likely. The second is outright theft, which also seems implausible, even for a man as complex as Nabokov. That forces us on to the remaining two, unconscious borrowing and deliberate quotation. Unconscious borrowing of a previously read text is a distinct possibility, given that Nabokov claimed that he often read several books a week and later 'forgot' them. It is common for authors to forget they have *not* invented phrases or situations which they then regurgitate in their own work. But to reproduce, unconsciously, something with this number of matches surely strains credulity. That leaves the last option: deliberate quotation of an admired predecessor. It is one of the more common literary strategies. Nabokov was certainly not above sly references, nor a stranger to obscure ones. One of the subtlest involves the quotation given above: 'Did she have a precursor? She did, indeed she did.' These are among the opening words of the novel *Lolita*, in which Humbert explains that his thirst for nymphets is an amatory hangover from his childhood, when he had loved, although never to the point of consummation, a girl called Annabel Leigh:

> She would try to relieve the pain of love by first roughly rubbing her dry lips against mine; then my darling would draw away with a nervous toss of her hair, and then again come darkly near and let me feed on her open

mouth, while with a generosity that was ready to offer her everything, my heart, my throat, my entrails, I gave her to hold in her awkward fist the scepter of my passion [. . .]

But that mimosa grove – the haze of stars, the tingle, the flame, the honeydew, and the ache remained with me, and that little girl with her seaside limbs and ardent tongue haunted me ever since – until at last, twenty-four years later, I broke her spell by incarnating her in another.

But 'Annabel Lee' is the heroine of a poem by Edgar Allan Poe (whose own child-bride was fourteen when he married her):

> I was a child and she was a child,
> In this kingdom by the sea;
> But we loved with a love that was more than love
> I and my Annabel Lee.

So Lolita did have a precursor, one whom 'he loved, one summer'. But it was a literary precursor. Replace the word 'loved' with the word 'read' (not such a gigantic shift for Nabokov, for whom the pleasure of the text was the most exquisite of all) and we get, possibly, a truer reflection of the state of affairs. Nabokov's nymphets were literary nymphets. 'Annabel Leigh' had her true origins in a work of the imagination. Was the inclusion of this 'certain initial girl-child' Nabokov's way of telling us that the same was true of her sister Lolita, and that lurking behind Lolita was a Nazi called Heinz von Lichberg?

44. CATCH-22
(1961)

'Catch-22' has passed into the language as a description of the impossible bind:

> Yossarian looked at him soberly and tried another approach. 'Is Orr crazy?'
>
> 'He sure is,' Doc Daneeka said.
>
> 'Can you ground him?'
>
> 'I sure can. But first he has to ask me to. That's part of the rule [. . .]'
>
> 'And then you can ground him?' Yossarian asked.
>
> 'No. Then I can't ground him.'
>
> 'You mean there's a catch?'
>
> 'Sure there's a catch,' Doc Daneeka replied. 'Catch-22. Anyone who wants to get out of combat duty isn't really crazy.'

Orr is crazy, and can be grounded, but if he asks to be grounded he is sane – and he can only be grounded if he asks. Joseph Heller complained that the phrase 'a Catch-22 situation' was often used by people who did not seem to understand what it meant. Given the mental contortions of the catch, this is not surprising. He even described receiving a letter from a Finnish translator, which said (in Heller's paraphrase in an interview): 'I am translating your novel *Catch-22* into Finnish. Would you please explain me one thing: What means *Catch-22*? I didn't find it in any vocabulary. Even assistant air attaché of the USA here in Helsinki could not explain exactly.' Heller added: 'I suspect the book lost a great deal in its Finnish translation.'

There are no catches 1 to 21, or 23 onwards, in the book. 'There was only one catch and that was Catch-22.' Like the final commandment left at the end of *Animal Farm*,[1] Catch-22 is an entire rule book distilled into one lunatic decree. Its very uniqueness meant that Heller had to think carefully before naming, or numbering it. And his choice was – Catch-18.

In the Second World War Heller was a bombardier with the 12th Air Force, based on Corsica, and flew sixty missions over Italy and France. Yossarian in *Catch-22* is a bombardier flying the same missions. Rotated home in 1945 and discharged as a First Lieutenant with an Air Medal with Five Oak Leaf Clusters, Heller took a degree at New York University, then an MA at Columbia, before working in New York as an advertising copywriter. In 1953 he began writing a book called *Catch-18*, the first chapter of which was published in the magazine *New World Writing* in 1955. When, three years later, he submitted the first large chunk of it to Simon & Schuster, it was quickly accepted for publication, and Heller worked on it steadily – all the time thinking of it as *Catch-18* – until its completion in 1961. Shortly before publication, however, the blockbuster novelist Leon Uris produced a novel entitled *Mila 18* (also about the Second World War). It was thought advisable that Heller, the first-time novelist, should be the one to blink. Heller said in an interview with *Playboy* in 1975: 'I was heartbroken. I thought 18 was the only number.' A long process of numerical agonizing began in which the author and his editor at Simon & Schuster, Robert Gottlieb, worked their way through the integers looking for the right, the unique formula. *Catch-11* was one of the first suggestions, but was rejected because of the film *Ocean's Eleven*. Heller at one point settled firmly on *Catch-14*, but Gottlieb threw it out for being too nondescript. When 22 came up Gottlieb felt it had the right ring: 'I thought 22 was a funnier number than 14,' he told the *New York Times Review of Books* in 1967. Heller took two weeks to persuade.

But the journey from 18 to 22, although tortuous, was worth making. The reason is this: 22 has a thematic significance that 18 and most of the other choices do not.

The doubling of the digits emphasized a major theme of the book: duplication and reduplication. When the book was first published, critics objected to its monotony and repetition. 'Heller's talent is impressive,' said *Time* magazine, 'but it is also undisciplined, sometimes luring him into bogs of boring repetition. Nearly every episode in *Catch-22* is told and retold.'

This is true. In *Catch-22* everything is doubled. Yossarian flies over the bridge at Ferrara twice, his food is poisoned twice, there is a chapter devoted to 'The Soldier Who Saw Everything Twice', the chaplain has the sensation of having experienced everything twice, Yossarian can name two things to be miserable about for every one to be thankful for, all Yossarian can say to the dying Snowden is 'There, there,' all Snowden can say is 'I'm cold, I'm cold,' Yossarian overhears a woman repeatedly begging 'please don't, please don't,' and Major Major is actually Major Major Major Major. The critic J.P. Stern identified a pairing approach to the characters:

> Most figures in Catch-22 are arranged in pairs; e.g., the medical orderlies Gus and Wes; the HR clerk Wintergreen and the Chaplain's orderly – both nasty characters; the two CID stooges; Major Major and Captain Flume – both persecuted; Generals Dreedle and Peckem – both harshly satirized; Snowden and Mudd – both dead; Piltchard and Wren – both enjoy combat missions; Aarfy and Black – men without feeling; Nately and Clevinger – upper-class college boys, both get killed; the nurses, Duckett and Kramer.[2]

The mad pairing reaches its apotheosis in the catch itself. As the novel says: 'Yossarian saw it clearly in all its spinning reasonableness. There was an elliptical precision about its perfect pairs of parts that was graceful and shocking, like good modern art, and at times Yossarian wasn't quite sure that he saw it at all, just the way he was never quite sure about good modern art . . .'

Doubling is thus a stylistic device suggestive of the qualified nature of reality. Nothing is singular, unblurred or unambiguous. The title, with its doubled digits (2 representing duality, itself doubled to make 22) conveys this in a way that *Catch-18* could never have done.

It seems clear therefore that what happened when Simon & Schuster found out about Leon Uris's book was a piece of great good luck.

1 'All animals are equal, but some animals are more equal than others.'
2 J.P. Stern, 'War and the Comic Muse: *The Good Soldier Schweik* and *Catch*-22', (1968)

45. WHO'S AFRAID
OF VIRGINIA WOOLF?
(1962)

By the early 1960s Edward Albee was unquestionably off-Broadway's hottest property. With *The Zoo Story*, his one-act absurdist drama of 1959, he was hailed as a home-grown Samuel Beckett. Further well-received one-acts included *The Death of Bessie Smith*, *The American Dream* and *The Sandbox*. But his first full-length play, *Who's Afraid of Virginia Woolf?* (and full-length it was – it went on for three hours), was something else entirely: a blockbuster sensation. At first greeted with shocked incomprehension ('a sick play for sick people'; 'for dirty-minded females only') it went on to win numerous major awards, transferred to Broadway, was made into a multi-Oscar-winning film (all four of its actors were nominated for Academy Awards, and in the event won two, for Best Actress and Best Supporting Actress), and took Europe by storm (in Prague it was billed as *Who's Afraid of Franz Kafka?*).

But the play was not 'absurdist' or particularly 'modernist'. It was in many ways a quite traditional exploration, in the manner of Strindberg, of what can happen when two articulate, educated people decide to tear chunks out of each other in front of guests. Its originality was that as a study in matrimonial attrition it went deeper, was more savage and uncompromising than anything yet seen in the American theatre. 'Total war' is the formula George and Martha agree on in Act Two; and in Act Three, George, humiliated and angry, avails himself of the atomic option. *Who's Afraid of Virginia Woolf?* was quite frighteningly merciless, and quite frighteningly hilarious.

The title was a major part of the play's success. It originated from 1954. Albee was in the habit of drinking at an establishment in Greenwich Village called 'The College of Complexes', and behind the bar was a large mirror on which patrons were free to scrawl messages in soap. One night he saw the legend 'Who's Afraid of Virginia Woolf?' and it amused him. It was to be eight years before it became a question that the whole of theatre-going New York was asking itself.

In the early stages of writing, the play was called *Exorcism*. 'Who's afraid of Virginia Woolf?' was merely a line in the play. The line later moved to become the play's subtitle, and then, at some point in the writing, with 'Exorcism' relegated to the third-act title (the first two acts are 'Fun and Games' and 'Walpurgisnacht') *Who's Afraid of Virginia Woolf?* became the main title. Albee said that its meaning was 'who's afraid of the big, bad wolf, which means who's afraid of living life without delusions?' Of the many delusions on offer in the play, the central one is the private game of the two main characters, college professor George and his ball-breaking wife Martha, who have invented a non-existent son. The main rule governing the game is that their son must never be mentioned in public. This is the rule that Martha breaks in Act One, by mentioning him to one of their guests. George, after a lacerating few hours, takes his revenge by killing the son:

GEORGE: Now listen, Martha; listen carefully. We got a telegram; there was a car accident, and he's dead. POUF! Just like that! Now, how do you like it?

MARTHA: [*a howl which weakens into a moan*]: NOOOOOOooooooo.

Martha must pay the price for her transgression. They must both now live without their delusion. The last lines of the play make the point:

GEORGE: [*puts his hand gently on her shoulder; she puts
    her head back and he sings to her, very softly*]: Who's
    afraid of Virginia Woolf
    Virginia Woolf
    Virginia Woolf,
MARTHA: I . . . am . . . George . . .
GEORGE: Who's afraid of Virginia Woolf . . .
MARTHA: I . . . am . . . George . . . I . . . am . . .
[GEORGE nods, slowly.]
[Silence; tableau]
CURTAIN

Strangely enough for a title with such a concrete starting
point, there was at least one other possible influence on it, in
the work of James Thurber, an author whom Albee admired
(and admires) greatly. Thurber was, to many, the greatest
twentieth-century observer of marital conflict, particularly in
his short stories: much of the dialogue of these pieces, in
which contests are played out between domineering wives
and resentful husbands, finds an echo in the private-language
bitching of Albee's play. There is 'The Curb in the Sky' ('He
always gets that line wrong'), 'Am I Not Your Rosalind?'
('Shut up, George, and give me some more ice') or 'Mr Pendly
and the Poindexter' ('What's the matter; are you in a trance,
or what?'). There is even a Thurber short story called 'The
Interview' in which the protagonists are a husband and wife
called George and Martha, and in which George, a writer,
gets drunk and taunts Martha, in front of a guest, over their
failing marriage. More pertinently as regards the title, in 1939
Thurber co-wrote, with Elliott Nugent, the play *The Male
Animal*. Its main character is Tommy Turner, a college professor (like George) with an emasculating wife (like Martha)
who is attracted to a younger football-player (like Nick, the
boxer and biology professor in *Who's Afraid of Virginia*

Woolf?). Turner wants to read to his class a letter by the anarchist Bartolomeo Vanzetti, but is warned by his wife that if he does so he risks being fired. He must make a decision either to stand up for himself or back down, and if he backs down he will very probably be cuckolded too. 'I won't,' he says. 'I'm scared of those Neanderthal men. I'll talk about football.' But then he sings: 'Who's afraid of the Big Bad Wolf? The Big Bad Wolf? The Big Bad Wolf?' Staking all on one throw, he reads the letter and is supported not only by his faculty but, surprisingly, by the football team.

A second possible influence came from the work of Virginia Woolf herself. In around 1962 Albee wrote to Leonard Woolf to ask him if it would be all right to use his wife's name as part of the title. Leonard Woolf said it would. Later, when the play transferred to the West End of London, Woolf went to see it with Peggy Ashcroft, and wrote to Albee: 'We both enjoyed it immensely. It is so amusing and at the same time moving and is really about the important things in life. Nothing is rarer, at any rate, on the English stage. I wonder if you have ever read a short story which my wife wrote and is printed in *A Haunted House?* It is called "Lappin and Lapinova". The details are quite different but the theme is the same as that of the imaginary child in your play.'[1] Leonard Woolf was perhaps being tactful. 'Lappin and Lapinova' is about a married couple who, in the absence of children of their own, invent a secret fantasy world. In it the husband is a rabbit and the wife a hare:

> Thus when they came back from their honeymoon they possessed a private world [. . .] No one guessed that there was such a place, and that of course made it all the more amusing. It made them feel, more even than most young married couples, in league together against the rest of the world [. . .] Without that world, how, Rosalind wondered, that winter could she have lived at all?

But the breakdown of the marriage leads to a breakdown of the shared fantasy, and it is dealt a cruel *coup de grâce* by the husband:

> 'It's Lapinova . . .' she faltered, glancing wildly at him out of her great startled eyes. 'She's gone, Ernest. I've lost her!'
>
> [. . .]
>
> 'Yes,' he said at length. 'Poor Lapinova . . .' He straightened his tie at the looking-glass over the mantel-piece.
>
> 'Caught in a trap,' he said, 'killed,' and sat down and read the newspaper.
>
> So that was the end of that marriage.

Albee claimed never to have read the short story.

1 In Mel Gussow, *Edward Albee: A Singular Journey* (1999)

46. A CLOCKWORK ORANGE
(1962)

A Clockwork Orange is set in an indeterminate near-future, by implication Britain, but with some resemblances to Soviet Russia. It is written in 'nadsat',[1] an invented language which mixes English with Russian loan-words, gypsy slang and Burgessisms. Alex and his droogs (friends) spend their evenings dratsing (fighting), crasting (robbing) shops to supply their need for the latest classical-music releases, and indulging in a bit of the old in-out in-out (rape). Alex finally overreaches himself and is put in prison, where he chooses to undergo a new rehabilitation treatment, the Ludovico technique (named after Ludwig/Ludovico van Beethoven?) in the hope of an early release. The Ludovico technique conditions him, in Pavlovian fashion, to react with nausea at any sign of violence. At the end of the book, Alex either ends up returning to his former ways or grows up and sees the error of them, according to which edition you read.[2]

Burgess gave at least three possible origins for the title *A Clockwork Orange*, none of them entirely convincing.

The first was that he had overheard the phrase 'as queer as a clockwork orange' in a London pub in 1945 and took it to be a Cockney expression. He wrote in the introduction to the 1987 US edition:

> I don't think I have to remind readers what the title means. Clockwork oranges don't exist, except in the speech of old Londoners. The image was a bizarre one, always used for a bizarre thing. 'He's as queer as a clockwork orange' meant he was queer to the limit of queerness. It did not primarily denote homosexuality, though

a queer, before restrictive legislation came in, was the term used for a member of the inverted fraternity.

Burgess claimed in a different essay, 'Clockwork Marmalade', published in the *Listener* in 1972, that he had heard the phrase several times since that first occasion, usually in the mouths of aged Cockneys. But no other record of the existence of any such expression in use before 1962 has surfaced. Several commentators have doubted whether it ever existed. Why a clockwork orange, in particular? Why not a clockwork apple? The phrase does not seem to have much wit or accuracy when describing something queer, odd or strange. There are no expressions about robot bananas or mechanical plums, probably for good reason.

The second explanation was that the title was a pun on the Malay word *orang*, meaning man.[3] Burgess taught in Malaysia (or Malaya as it then was) from 1954 to 1959, and was, by the end, fluent in Malay. He wrote in *Joysprick*, his study of Joyce:

> I myself was, for nearly six years, in such close touch with the Malay language that it affected my English and still affects my thinking. When I wrote a novel called *A Clockwork Orange*, no European reader saw that the Malay word for 'man' – orang – was contained in the title (Malay students of English invariably write 'orang squash') . . .

This conjuring of a clockwork man, central to the novel's ideas, is clever, but sounds like an afterthought. Burgess wrote elsewhere that the *orang* echo was a 'secondary' meaning – which is probably shorthand for a happy accident. The novel contains nothing else identifiably Malay.

This leads into the third possibility, which is, as he wrote in the prefatory note to *A Clockwork Orange: A Play with Music*, that the title is a metaphor for an organic entity, full of juice and sweetness and agreeable odour, being turned into an automaton.

This idea is strongly built into the book. The story of Alex is one in which two unpleasant alternatives for future societies are contrasted. The first is one in which malefactors are allowed to exercise free will to torture and murder, and are, if caught, punished; the second is one in which they have their freedom of choice cauterized by the Ludovico technique, resulting in a safe society populated by automata. Burgess intended to contrast two ways of looking at the world, the Augustinian and the Pelagian. The Augustinian position is that man's freedom is guaranteed, but that original sin makes suffering inevitable. The Pelagian (and heretical) view is that mankind is perfectible and that original sin can be overridden. Augustinianism is associated with the politically conservative idea that people will inevitably behave badly, but that freedom is God-given and must not be fundamentally tampered with; Pelagianism is associated with communist or fascist regimes (or even wishy-washy liberal ones) which offer an earthly paradise but demand obedience, even at the level of thought and feeling. Throughout his fiction Burgess leant heavily towards the Augustinian side of the debate. The phrase 'a clockwork orange', as representative of the Pelagian nightmare, appears in the book itself, in fact as the title of a book. Alex and his gang break into the house of a writer and Alex notices a manuscript:

'It's a book,' I said. 'It's a book what you are writing.' I made the old goloss very coarse. 'I have always had the strongest admiration for them as can write books.' Then I looked at its top sheet, and there was the name – A CLOCKWORK ORANGE – and I said: 'That's a fair gloopy title. Who ever heard of a clockwork orange?' Then I read a malenky bit out loud in a sort of very high preaching goloss: 'The attempt to impose upon man, a creature of growth and capable of sweetness, to ooze juicily at the last round the bearded lips of God, to attempt to impose, I say, laws and conditions appropriate to a mechanical creation, against this I raise my sword-pen.'

A Clockwork Orange, as a text, is a theme waiting for a title, which makes the third explanation the most persuasive. But it does not really answer the question of why that particular title.

So: it may be a Cockney expression, may be an echo of a Malay word, or may simply have been suggested by the book's themes. There is one other possibility, however. Did Burgess mishear that conversation in the pub?

Terry's began manufacturing its Chocolate Orange in 1931. Previously there had been a Chocolate Apple, but the Chocolate Orange began to outsell it, and the Chocolate Apple was withdrawn in 1954. There was also, at one point, an experiment with a Chocolate Lemon. The words 'chocolate orange' were thus a part of everyday speech in 1940s London, and might have been overheard anywhere. 'Chocolate' and 'clockwork' are not homophones, but they are close, and might sound alike in a noisy pub. Perhaps Burgess misheard. Perhaps he even realized that he had misheard but liked what he had misheard. Perhaps – I speculate – he did not want to admit to the drab mercantile origins of his title.

1 From the Russian suffix meaning 'teen'.
2 The British Heinemann edition included a final 21st chapter in which Alex repents his ways and graduates to more sophisticated musical styles such as *lieder*. The US Norton edition omitted the chapter, and the book ended with Alex unrepentantly planning more crimes from his hospital bed. Needless to say the moral/theological thrust of the book is entirely different according to which edition is read.
3 The Malay *orang-utan* means 'man of the woods'.

47. THE HOMECOMING
(1965)

MAX: They come back from America, they bring the slop-
    bucket with them. They bring the bedpan with them.
    (To TEDDY.) Take that disease away from me. Get her
    away from me.
TEDDY: She's my wife!
MAX: (To JOEY.) Chuck them out.

Such is the filth and the fury of Harold Pinter's *The Homecoming*. Teddy, a college professor, and Ruth, his wife, have
returned unexpectedly from America to Teddy's family home
in the East End of London. The house is inhabited by Teddy's
father Max (a tyrant in cloth cap and plimsolls), his paternal
uncle Sam (a chauffeur and dogsbody) and his brothers Lenny
(a sharp-suited pimp) and Joey (a thick-headed boxer). They
have not seen Teddy for nine years, and are unaware that he is
married.

As the action develops, a primordial struggle takes place in
which Ruth, the only woman, is pitted against the other characters. She seduces Joey, although he is not permitted to 'go the
whole hog'; she coolly undermines Lenny, who has attempted
to intimidate her with tales of his violent assaults on two
women; Max she reduces to a stumbling, wounded old man
begging for a kiss (despite his earlier, rather unwelcoming atti-
tude); and Sam she merely ignores, aware of his status as a
powerless bystander. The play ends, astoundingly, with her
giving up her place as the wife of an American college lecturer
for the life of a prostitute in a Soho flat (provided by Lenny).
She also appears to give consideration to the idea that her
duties will include the sexual servicing of Max, Lenny and Joey.

In his plays Pinter often draws on personal experience or on the experiences of those close to him.[1] The events of *The Homecoming* are paralleled in events that took place in the life of a childhood friend, Morris Wernick.

In the mid-1950s Wernick, a Jewish East Ender, left his home and went to Canada, where he became a Professor of English at Montreal University. Shortly before leaving, he married, but kept the marriage secret. His wife was not Jewish, and he feared that his father would be unable to accept her as part of the family. Much later Wernick wrote to Michael Billington, the drama critic and biographer of Pinter:

> I married in 1956 and left immediately to start life in Canada. I never told my father that I was married and for the next ten years continued to keep up this 'pretence' even on my infrequent visits to England. Harold thought this action on my part unwise, as did Henry, Joe Brearley, my wife and, come to think of it, everyone except me. They all went along with it out of respect for my wishes. I came, in time, to join the ranks of those who felt that it was ridiculous and in 1964 I brought my whole family to England where my father met his daughter-in-law and grandchildren. I do not need to tell you that it was one of the memorable moments in my life. Why did I take what I now regard as a mistaken course? For the simple reason that I believed it would spare him being hurt. Forty years ago marrying 'out' was still not regarded lightly. My father was in no sense a bigot and I certainly did not live in fear of his displeasure. Harold would get a laugh out of this idea, as would anyone who knew him.

Morris Wernick returned in 1964, the year before the play was completed. Pinter unquestionably based *The Homecoming* on the potentialities inherent in the Wernick ménage:

he even sent Wernick a first draft of the play. The correspondences run even deeper. Pinter acknowledged that Max was drawn, in part, from Wernick's father. Wernick also had two brothers – as in the play – as well as an uncle who was a cabbie. These are of course starting points: there is no suggestion that Wernick's brother was a pimp, or that the family all ended up giving Wernick's wife 'a walk round the park'. These were Pinter's additions. But the homecoming of *The Homecoming* nevertheless drew heavily on real events.

There was, however, another possible influence.

In an interview that took place in Egypt in 1967, Joe Orton made some revealing comments about *The Homecoming*. He recorded them in his diary of July 11:

> We talked of Pinter. His work isn't known in Egypt. Not surprisingly Harold being Jewish. [The interviewer] asked if *Entertaining Mr Sloane* was on before *The Homecoming*. 'Oh, yes,' I said. 'Two years before.' 'The similarities are overwhelming,' he said. He thought perhaps Harold had seen *Sloane* and been influenced by it in the second act of *The Homecoming*. 'I'm sure he did,' I said. '*The Homecoming* couldn't have been written without *Sloane*. And, you know, in a way the second act – although I admire it very much – isn't true. Harold, I'm sure, would never share anyone sexually. I would.'

Entertaining Mr Sloane in fact received its premiere one year before *The Homecoming*, in May 1964. It does show some interesting prefigurations of Pinter's play. In *Entertaining Mr Sloane* we get a species of homecoming – the protagonist, Sloane, is returning to the scene of a murder. His return sets off a power struggle in a sordid London house. It ends with a body on the floor (Kemp, and Sam in *The Homecoming*) and one character (Sloane/Ruth) being sexually shared by the rest of the cast. It is a little as if Pinter had taken Wernick's story for the first act and grafted on the unpleasant parts of *Sloane* for the second.

It has been said that there are only ten plots. Perhaps the return of the prodigal, and the sexual sharing of said prodigal or his wife with the rest of the cast, is one of them.

1 There are numerous examples of this: one would be *The Hothouse*, which was based partly on Pinter's participation in medical experiments at the Maudsley Hospital in 1954.

48. THE SCUM MANIFESTO
(1967)

At around 4 o' clock in the afternoon on June 3, 1968, Valerie Solanas attempted to kill her friend Andy Warhol. Her first two shots missed ('I should have done target practice,' she commented later) but the third shot ripped through both his lungs and left him close to death. She then turned the gun on an art curator, Mario Amaya, who happened to be waiting to see Warhol that day at the Factory Studio in New York. Again she missed, but hit him in the hip with her second shot. Placing the gun to the head of a third man, Warhol's manager Fred Hughes, she pulled the trigger, but the gun jammed. Solanas then left the building. Later she turned herself in to a traffic policeman.

It was not, perhaps, very surprising. Valerie Solanas was the author of the *SCUM Manifesto*, and '*SCUM*' stood, it was claimed, for 'Society for Cutting Up Men'.[1] The manifesto called for the destruction of the male sex. 'Life in this society being, at best, an utter bore and no aspect of society being at all relevant to women, there remains to civic-minded, responsible, thrill-seeking females only to overthrow the government, eliminate the money system, institute complete automation and destroy the male sex,' she wrote, in what must be one of the most high-octane opening sentences of any book ever written. The book went on to discuss war, money, marriage, prostitution, fatherhood, mental illness, domesticity, religion, Great Art, censorship and automation (of which Solanas was warmly in favour), and closed 50 breathtaking pages later, again with a memorable piece of polemic:

> Rational men want to be squashed, stepped on, crushed and crunched, treated as the curs, the filth that they are, have their repulsiveness confirmed.

The sick, irrational men, those who attempt to defend themselves against their disgustingness, when they see SCUM barrelling down on them, will cling in terror to Big Mama with her Big Bouncy Boobies, but Boobies won't protect them against SCUM; Big Mama will be clinging to Big Daddy, who will be in the corner shitting in his forceful, dynamic pants. Men who are rational, however, won't kick or struggle or raise a distressing fuss, but will just sit back, relax, enjoy the show and ride the waves to their demise.

The book had been written in 1967 and self-published in mimeographed copies which Valerie hawked on the streets. Warhol recognized her talent and thought her amusing – and, disturbing though the *SCUM Manifesto* is, it is also, in parts, hilarious, and intentionally so. She began to work with Warhol on various projects, acting in his film *I, A Man*. Her writing career seemed to be picking up when Maurice Girodias of the Olympia Press paid her an advance of $600 for the rights to an autobiographical novel.

Then things turned sour. She began arguing with Girodias and Warhol. The former had not seen anything for his $600; Solanas angrily told him he could have the *Manifesto* instead, and do what he liked with it. She accused Warhol of not returning a script she had sent him, *Up Your Ass*. Her first thought was to get Girodias, and with this in mind she borrowed enough money to buy a .32 automatic pistol. After failing to find Girodias at home that June afternoon, she turned on Warhol. At her trial in 1969 she was indicted for 'recklessly endangering life', and, because Warhol refused to pursue the case, was given only three years in prison. Two months after the shootings, while Solanas was confined to a psychiatric ward, Girodias released the Olympia Press version of her book, which he called *S.C.U.M. (Society for Cutting Up Men) MANIFESTO.*

Warhol survived, badly injured, and never fully recovered his health. Nine years after the attempted assassination, in 1977, an unrepentant[2] Solanas was back on the streets, again selling a self-published version of her manifesto, this time in protest against what she saw as Girodias's defective version of the text. She called it the *SCUM Manifesto*, with the acronym not spelled out, and with no full stops after the letters of *SCUM*. This was the title used for all subsequent editions. In fact, even in earlier versions of the book, 'The Society for Cutting Up Men' had not been not mentioned anywhere in the text. SCUM was simply SCUM. It may have started life as an acronym, but that was not how Valerie later wanted to present it. SCUM was the voice of those women, like Valerie, an enraged, impoverished loner-lesbian, outside any group or any society, who were the rejected, the dregs, the refuse, the outcast. The scum, in fact. The spelling out of her coded title by Girodias was one more act of patriarchal intervention, an attempt to possess.[3] 'It's just a literary device,' Solanas said of SCUM in a 1977 interview. 'There's no organization called SCUM . . . It's not even me . . . I mean, I thought of it as a state of mind. In other words, women who think a certain way are in SCUM.' SCUM was so much more than the mere butchery of men. As the manifesto made clear, SCUM was 'out to destroy the system':

> SCUM will keep on destroying, looting, fucking-up and killing until the money-work system no longer exists and automation is completely instituted or until enough women co-operate with SCUM to make violence unnecessary to achieve these goals, that is, until enough women either unwork or quit work, start looting, leave men and refuse to obey all laws inappropriate to a truly civilized society.

The manifesto, like many other works composed on the brink of sanity, or in a howling rage, is not a coherent political programme, and, perhaps consciously, contained within it the recipe for SCUM's own disintegration. 'The conflict, therefore, is not between females and males, but between SCUM,' she wrote in the conclusion to the manifesto, using SCUM, as per usual, as an uncountable noun. 'SCUM is too impatient to wait for the de-brainwashing of millions of assholes. Why should the swinging females continue to plod dismally along with the dull male ones?' Dissenting, unswinging females had become 'male' females, and the fate of males was, of course, sealed. Internecine warfare had arrived in the cosmic death throes of the SCUM apocalypse. And SCUM will turn on SCUM. The future of humanity itself was in question. ('Why produce even females? Why should there be future generations? What is their purpose?') As in militant movements and terrorist cells everywhere, only the purest of the pure were finally considered God's (or Goddess's) elect. Valerie had written herself into a corner. SCUM had narrowed down to one woman, yet ballooned in significance until it took in all of her vast, unfocused rage against everyone, male and female alike.

1 Witty acronyms were beloved of feminist groups of the 1960s and 1970s. Among them were NOW (the National Organization of Women), WITCH (Women's International Terrorist Conspiracy from Hell) and APOASR (A Political Organization to Annihilate Sex Roles; you have to say it out loud). Andy Warhol satirized the tendency with a fictional organization, PIG (Politically-Involved Girlies).

2 She said of the shooting in 1977: 'I consider that a moral act. And I consider it immoral that I missed.'

3 The appropriation of titular rights by male publishers over female authors had been played out three hundred years earlier, when Anne Bradstreet's collection of poems had been published without her knowledge as *The Tenth Muse Lately Sprung Up in America* – a seventeenth-century example of publisher's hype: see chapter 8.

49. THE DECAY OF THE ANGEL
(1971)

One of the most revealing anecdotes about Yukio Mishima is as follows. One day in the late 1960s, when Mishima was at the height of his fame, a young man appeared outside his house in Tokyo. The family and servants soon saw him and realized that he was a literary pilgrim who wished to speak to the writer, but did not dare approach the door: his waiting outside was a standard way of soliciting an introduction. Mishima did not immediately ask the young man in, but instead kept him waiting for several hours to test his resolution. Finally, as evening approached, a maid was sent out to the youth with a message that he would be granted a brief interview. He was shown into the study, where Mishima told him: 'I don't have much time, so I am afraid I can only allow you one question. Now, what is it?' The young man paused and then asked respectfully: 'Master, when are you going to kill yourself?'

Yukio Mishima was born in 1925 and grew up in the period before the Second World War. He was sixteen when the war began, and lived his late teenage years in the expectation of conscription and violent death. But he flunked his army medical and spent the latter part of the war working in a factory. Survival, and the end of the war, he experienced as disaster. 'For me – me alone – it meant that fearful days were beginning,' he wrote. 'It meant that, whether I would or no, and despite everything that had deceived me into believing such a day would never come to pass, the very next day I must begin my life as an ordinary member of society. How the mere words made me tremble!'

As the war ended there was a spate of suicides, mainly among military leaders, but also among civilians, one of whom was the writer Hasuda, a friend of Mishima. Hasuda had written: 'I believe one should die young in this age. To die young, I am sure, is the culture of my country.' Mishima would not have disagreed. Many of the novels, plays and short stories he later produced are preoccupied by the idea of suicide and violent, young death. The persistence of the theme makes one suspect that it was not just the war that shaped this element of his psyche. He wrote in *Confessions of a Mask* that from an early age 'My heart's leaning towards Death and Night and Blood would not be denied.'

Hara-kiri, or, as it is also known in Japan, *seppuku*, is especially prominent in his fiction. *Seppuku* is the ancient ritualized form of self-killing involving the cutting open of one's own belly, usually in tandem with an accomplice called a *kaishaku* who delivers a decapitating sword-blow. In Mishima's short story 'Patriotism', a young army officer commits *seppuku*: his death is presented as a spiritual triumph. Mishima later starred in the film version of 'Patriotism', in which he acted out the *seppuku* scene. In the film *Hitogiri*, Mishima played the part of a samurai who commits *seppuku*. In the last year of his life he commissioned a photographer to take pictures of him faking *seppuku*. And in his novel *Runaway Horses* the main character commits *seppuku*. All of these suicides were of young men with firm, beautiful flesh: Mishima was bisexual, and his fascination with *seppuku* had an undoubted homoerotic aspect. He was a fanatical body builder, and in the essay 'Sun and Steel' he candidly outlined the reasons, linking physical beauty with death: 'Specifically, I cherished a romantic impulse towards death, yet at the same time I required a strictly classical body as its vehicle.'

The death thus predicted by his fiction occurred on November 25, 1970. It was part of a carefully engineered drama. Mishima had spent the last two years training a private army, the *Tate no kai* (Shield Society). It was with a detachment of five of these *Tate no kai* that he occupied the administrative headquarters of the army in Tokyo, taking a senior general hostage. Mishima demanded that the soldiers of the nearby bar-racks assemble to listen to him speak, or he would kill the general. When a crowd of several hundred had formed, Mishima came out on to a high balcony and harangued them for several minutes, calling on them to rise and overthrow the constitution. He was met with laughter and jeers. He then went inside, and, stripping to the waist and kneeling down, thrust a foot-long dagger into his belly. As he gasped on the carpet, com-pleting the cross-cut that would disgorge his entrails, he was beheaded by one of his men acting as *kaishaku*. A second soldier then knelt in turn, and was himself beheaded by another of the soldiers.

Mishima's death was greeted with incredulity in Japan, where *seppuku* had become virtually unknown since the end of the war. No one, it seemed, had taken his many graphic predic-tions of his own death seriously. But his last book went some way to explaining what had happened. This was *The Decay of the Angel*. The deadline for the final instalment of this work was November 25, 1970, the day on which he had killed himself. It had been duly completed and mailed that morning. The date that appears on the last line of the novel is also 'November 25, 1970'.

The Decay of the Angel is the last book in Mishima's longest work, the tetralogy *The Sea of Fertility*.[1] The series uses the notion of reincarnation as a structuring device. In each of the books, a young man dies at the age of twenty, and is then reincarnated in the subsequent volume. The main protagonist of all four books, Honda, comes to know each of the reincar-nations, recognizing each by a small formation of moles under the arm. The book's title in Japanese is *Tennin Gosui*, which lit-erally means *Five Signs of the Decay of the Tennin*: a *tennin* in Buddhist theology is a supernatural being roughly equivalent to a Christian angel, but vulnerable to death. The signs or omens of a *tennin*'s decline, five in number,[2] give the book its title.

Mishima's contention in *The Decay of the Angel* is that eternal beauty is the prize of those who 'cut time short', and that in order to achieve a beautiful life, one must die a beautiful and young death, before decay has set in. Honda, who has missed his chance to do this, meditates:

> Some are all the same endowed with the faculty to cut time short at the pinnacle. I know it to be true, for I have seen examples with my own eyes.
>
> What power, poetry, bliss! To be able to cut it short, just as the white radiance of the pinnacle comes into view ...
>
> Endless physical beauty. That is the special prerogative of those who cut time short. Just before the pinnacle when time must be cut short is the pinnacle of physical beauty.
>
> Clear, bright beauty, in the knowledge that the radiant white pinnacle lies ahead.

The meaning of the title is clear. Mishima himself was the angel threatened by decay. He knew that the death signs were slowly becoming visible on his body, that the flesh was becoming corrupt. Mishima believed that writing could only do so much. The body had its own urgent language, one inexpressible in words. His *seppuku* was a carefully orchestrated gathering of forces, sexual, aesthetic, political, literary, all converging on that same morning in November, with the aim of fixing beauty for ever.

---

1 The first three are *Spring Snow*, *Runaway Horses* and *The Temple of Dawn*.
2 The five signs are (although there are several variants): 'the flowers in the hair fade, a fetid sweat comes from under the arms, the robes are soiled, the body ceases to give off light, it loses awareness of itself.'

50. OLEANNA
(1992)

There is no character called Oleanna in *Oleanna*, nor is the name ever mentioned. There are only two people in Mamet's play: John, an American college professor, and Carol, his student. The action deals with an accusation of rape – which may or may not be justified – brought by Carol against John, and the threat to John's career that results. The play reaches its brutal culmination as John physically assaults Carol and knocks her to the floor, flinging misogynistic taunts at her. On the first performances of the play, in the febrile atmosphere following the Anita Hill–Clarence Thomas sexual harassment case in 1991, audiences were so stirred (the men rooting for John and the women for Carol) that fights broke out in the auditorium. The reviewer for the *New York Times* said it left him feeling 'soiled and furious'. When it was later filmed, cinema audiences reportedly cheered as John battered Carol.

But few members of the audience had any idea of why it was called *Oleanna*.

The title was in fact a remarkably obscure allusion to a nineteenth-century Utopian community in Pennsylvania called Oleana (one 'n'), after its Norwegian founder, Ole Bull (1810–80), a famous violinist, and his mother Anna (Ole + Anna = Oleana).

Ole Bull was ranked second only to Paganini in the nineteenth century's pantheon of violin virtuosi. His signature trick was to play on all four strings at once (he had a special flat bridge made for him for this purpose), and his improvisations on popular melodies were so rapid and difficult that one commentator said he seemed to be 'wrestling with the inward spasms of a Pythian frenzy'. Bull's friends included most of the century's writers and artists, women wrote to him asking for samples of his bath water, and he was the major inspiration behind the career of Edvard Grieg. After a triumphant concert tour of the USA in 1852 Bull decided to leave a permanent mark on the continent by purchasing 11,000 acres of land in Potter County, Pennsylvania, as a settlement for Norwegian immigrants.

Bull's fiefdom had four main settlements: Oleana, New Bergen, New Norway and New Valhalla. Pioneers flooded in, attracted by the prospect of free land, but it soon became clear that most of the 11,000 acres, located in a narrow valley between thickly forested hills, were completely unsuitable for farming. Bull's agent in the deal had been a local realtor, John F. Cowan, who had apparently neglected to mention this fact to his client. As it later turned out, even the arable land had been reserved by Cowan for his own use and had been left out of the contract. Bull was, at the very least, guilty of incompetence: perhaps he had also been swindled. The community failed. By the mid-1850s the colonists had either returned to their old homes or sought new homes elsewhere in the USA. Bull also returned, disillusioned, to Norway, and died in Bergen.

The debacle inspired a satirical folk song called 'Oleanna', originally composed in Norwegian and later recorded in a translation by Pete Seeger, as follows:

> Oh to be in Oleanna,
> That's where I'd like to be
> Than to be in Norway
> And bear the chains of slavery.
>
> Little roasted piggies
> Rush around the city streets
> Inquiring so politely
> If a slice of ham you'd like to eat.

Beer as sweet as Muncheners
Springs from the ground and flows away
The cows all like to milk themselves
And the hens lay eggs ten times a day.

Mamet included the first verse of this song as the epigraph to the printed version of his play.

The most immediate connection is to do with land. In *Oleanna* John spends much of the time on the phone to his wife or his lawyer talking about the purchase of a new house, while Carol, mute and waiting, listens. Something is wrong with the deeds, we learn: one of the easements threatens the purchase. Significantly, the very first words of the play are to do with 'the land':

JOHN (*on phone*) And what about the land. (*Pause*) The land. And what about the land? (*Pause*) What about it? (*Pause*) No. I don't understand [. . .] I'll be there, I'm sure I'll be there in fifteen, in twenty. I intend to. No, we aren't *going* to lose the, we aren't *going* to lose the house. Look: Look, I'm not minimizing it. The 'easement'. Did she say 'easement'? (*Pause*) What did she *say; is* it a 'term of art', are we *bound* by it . . . I'm sorry (*Pause*) are: we: yes.

Both John and Ole Bull's plans are eventually blighted by legal restrictions on the purchase of land. But John's failure to negotiate the sale of land, and Ole Bull's failure to pioneer a new Utopia, are paralleled, in the play, by another failure: the failure of the Utopian project of university education. John admits to Carol in a careless moment that he regards the whole university system as flawed and worthless, and that he is willing to break the rules and give her an 'A' grade, even though her work has been poor. He has the power to do it, and so why not? 'We won't tell anybody,' he says. Carol is shocked, puzzled, and finally outraged at the failure of the university system to supply what she has a right to expect: legitimate instruction, value for money. She berates John rather as a Norwegian colonist might have addressed Ole Bull – she has no 'security'; as in the song, she is a 'slave':

> CAROL . . . But to the aspirations of your students. Of *hard-working students*, who come here, who *slave* to come here – you have no idea what it cost me to come to this school – you *mock* us.
>
> [. . .]
>
> CAROL . . . But we worked to get to this school [. . .]To gain admittance here. To pursue that same degree of security *you* pursue. We, who, who are, at any moment, in danger of being deprived of it.

One might bear in mind that *Glengarry Glen Ross*, Mamet's play of 1984, is about real-estate agents who swindle members of the public by selling worthless parcels of land, and Mamet himself worked briefly for a real-estate company in the 1960s. *Oleanna*, it seems, picks up where *Glengarry Glen Ross* left off, exploring the inability of capitalism to ensure ethical social behaviour and the ever-present danger of getting royally ripped off. In both *Oleanna* and *Glengarry Glen Ross* there are dangerous people willing to bend the rules for their own ends. This is the meaning of *Oleanna* as a title: in the USA of David Mamet, the dream of security and social mobility through education and hard work is just another fantasy exploited by the unscrupulous to trap the gullible.

SOURCES AND FURTHER READING

Items are presented in order of the chapter they refer to.
Primary texts are given at the beginning of each paragraph.

Plato: *The Republic* (translation and introduction by H.D.P. Lee, Penguin, 1955)

More, Sir Thomas: *Utopia* (translation and introduction by Paul Turner, Penguin, 1965)
Kautsky, Karl: *Thomas More and his Utopia* (Russell & Russell, 1959)

Rabelais, François: *Gargantua and Pantagruel* (translation and introduction by J.M. Cohen, Penguin, 1955)
Screech, M.A.: *Rabelais* (Duckworth, 1979)

Sidney, Sir Philip: *Astrophel and Stella* (introduction by Alfred Pollard, David Stott, 1888)
Brother Anthony of Taizé: *Literature in English Society Before 1660: A Historical Survey* (Sogang University Press, 1998)
Stewart, Alan: *Philip Sidney: A Double Life* (Pimlico, 2001)

Marlowe, Christopher: *The Complete Plays* (introduction by J.B. Steane, Penguin, 1985)
Palmer, Philip Mason, and More, Robert Pattison: *The Sources of the Faust Tradition from Simon Magus to Lessing* (Octagon, 1966)
Thomas, Vivien, and Tydeman, William: *Christopher Marlowe: The Plays and their Sources* (Routledge, 1994)

Shakespeare, William: *Hamlet* (edited by Ann Thompson and Neil Taylor, Thomson Learning, 2006)
Greenblatt, Stephen: *Will in the World: How Shakespeare became Shakespeare* (Norton, 2004)
Hadfield, Andrew: 'The *Ur-Hamlet* and the Fable of the Kid', *Notes and Queries*, Vol. 53, No. 1 (2006)
Hansen, William F.: *Saxo Grammaticus and the Life of Hamlet* (University of Nebraska Press, 1983)

Jump, John, ed.: *Hamlet: A Casebook* (Macmillan, 1968)

Webster, John: *The Duchess of Malfi* (Dover, 1999)
Boklund, Gunnar, *The Duchess of Malfi: Sources, Themes, Characters* (Harvard University Press, 1962)

Bradstreet, Anne: *Poems* (introduction by Robert Hutchinson, Dover, 1969)
Piercy, Josephine K.: *Anne Bradstreet* (Twayne, 1965)

Perrault, Charles: *Histories or Tales of Past Times Told by Mother Goose with Morals* (Fortune Press, 1928)
Barchilon, Jacques and Flinders, Peter: *Charles Perrault* (Twayne, 1981)
Dundes, Alan, ed., *Cinderella: A Casebook* (University of Winconsin Press, 1982)

Pope, Alexander: *The Rape of the Lock* (edited by Elizabeth Gurr, Oxford University Press, 1990)
Hunt, John Dixon, ed.: *The Rape of the Lock: A Casebook* (Macmillan, 1968)
Rousseau, G.S., ed.: *Twentieth Century Interpretations of 'The Rape Of The Lock': A Collection of Critical Essays* (Prentice-Hall, 1969)
Williams, Abigail: 'John Ozell', *Oxford Dictionary of National Biography* (Oxford University Press, 2004)

Fielding, Henry: *An Apology for the Life of Mrs. Shamela Andrews* (introduction by Sheridan W. Baker, University of California Press, 1953)
Fielding, Henry: *Shamela* (introduction by Thomas Keymer, Oxford World's Classics, 1999)
Turner, James Grantham: 'Novel Panic: Picture and Performance in the Reception of Richardson's Pamela', *Representations*, No. 48 (1994)

Cleland, John: *Memoirs of a Woman of Pleasure* (introduction and notes by Peter Sabor, Oxford University Press, 1985)
Epstein, William Henry: *John Cleland: Images of a Life* (Columbia University Press, 1975)

Green, Jonathon: 'Dating Slang on "Historical Principles"', *Revue d'Études Françaises*, No. 11 (2006)

Wyss, Johann David: *The Swiss Family Robinson* (Oxford University Press, 1922)
Gove, Philip Babcock: *The Imaginary Voyage in Prose Fiction* (Holland Press, 1961)

Shelley, Mary: *Frankenstein* (introduction and notes by Maurice Hindle, Penguin, 1992)
Bennett, Betty T, ed.: *The Letters of Mary Wollstonecraft Shelley* (Johns Hopkins University Press, 1980)
Florescu, Radu: *In Search of Frankenstein* (Robson Books, 1996)
Ozolins, Aija: 'Recent Work on Mary Shelley and Frankenstein', *Science Fiction Studies*, Vol. 3, No. 2 (1976)
Seymour, Miranda: *Mary Shelley* (Picador, 2001)

Brontë, Charlotte, Emily and Anne: *Poems* (Black, 1985: facsimile of *Poems by Currer, Ellis and Acton Bell*, 1846)
Gérin, Winifred: *The Brontës* (Harlow, 1973)
Thormahlen, Marianne: 'The Brontë Pseudonyms', *English Studies*, Vol. 75, No. 3 (1994)

Browning, Elizabeth Barrett: *Sonnets from the Portuguese* (Dover, 1992)
Gosse, Edmund: *Critical Kit-Kats* (Heinemann, 1896)
Taplin, Gardner B.: *The Life of Elizabeth Barrett Browning* (John Murray, 1957)

Dumas *fils*, Alexandre: *La Dame aux Camélias* (translation and introduction by David Coward, Oxford World's Classics, 1986)
Saunders, Edith: *The Prodigal Father* (Longmans, Green & Co., 1951)

Wordsworth, William: *The Prelude* (introduction and notes by P.M. Yarker, Routledge, 1968)
Herford, C.H.: *Wordsworth* (Routledge, 1930)

Melville, Herman: *Moby-Dick* (introduction and notes by Harold Beaver, Penguin, 1972)

Browning, Robert: *The Ring and the Book* (introduction by
Richard D. Altick, Penguin, 1971)
Thomas, Donald: *Robert Browning* (Weidenfeld & Nicholson,
1982)
Ward, Maisie: *Robert Browning and his World* (Cassell, 1969)

Verne, Jules: *Around The World In Eighty Days* (Viking, 1996)
Costello, Peter: *Jules Verne, Inventor of Science Fiction* (Hodder
and Stoughton, 1978)
Wallace, Irving: *The Square Pegs* (Hutchinson, 1958)

Conan Doyle, Arthur: *A Study in Scarlet* (Penguin, 1981)
Edwards, Owen Dudley: *The Quest for Sherlock Holmes*
(Mainstream, 1983)
Stashower, Daniel: *Teller of Tales: The Life of Arthur Conan Doyle*
(Penguin, 2000)

Tolstoy, Leo: *The Kreutzer Sonata and Other Stories* (introduction
and notes by David McDuff, Penguin, 1985)
Tolstoy, Leo: *The Kreutzer Sonata and Other Stories* (introduction
by Doris Lessing, Modern Library, 2003)
Troyat, Henri: *Tolstoy* (Penguin, 1967)

Wilde, Oscar: *The Picture of Dorian Gray* (Penguin, 1985)
McCormack, Jerusha Hull: *The Man Who Was Dorian Gray*
(St Martin's Press, 2000)

Chekhov, Anton: *Selected Works* (Progress, 1979)
Hellman, Lillian, ed.: *The Selected Letters of Anton Chekhov*
(Hamish Hamilton, 1955)
Troyat, Henri: *Chekhov* (Macmillan, 1987)

Jarry, Alfred: *The Ubu Plays* (introduction by Kenneth McLeish,
Nick Hern Books, 1997)
Beaumont, Keith: *Alfred Jarry: A Critical and Biographical Study*
(Leicester University Press, 1984)

Synge, J.M.: *The Playboy of the Western World* (Dover, 1993)
Benson, Eugene: *J.M. Synge* (Macmillan, 1982)
Kilroy, James: *The 'Playboy' Riots* (Dolmen, 1971)

Stopes, Marie: *Married Love* (Oxford, 2004)
Hall, Ruth: *Marie Stopes* (Virago, 1977)
Rose, June: *Marie Stopes and the Sexual Revolution* (Faber, 1992)

Wodehouse, P.G.: *My Man Jeeves* (Wildside, 2004)
Donaldson, Frances: *P.G. Wodehouse* (Futura, 1982)
Usborne, Richard: *Wodehouse at Work to the End* (Penguin, 1976)
http://content-uk.cricinfo.com/ci/content/player/15666.html

Joyce, James: *Ulysses* (introduction and notes by Jeri Johnson,
    Oxford World's Classics, 1993)
Ellmann, Richard: *James Joyce* (Oxford University Press, 1959)
Ellmann, Richard: *Selected Letters of James Joyce* (Faber, 1975)
Owen, Rodney Wilson: *James Joyce and the Beginnings of* Ulysses
    (UMI Research Press, 1983)

Eliot, T.S.: *The Annotated Waste Land* (edited by Lawrence Rainey,
    Yale University Press, 2005)
Cox, C.B., and Hinchliffe, Arnold P, eds: *The Waste Land: A
    Casebook* (Macmillan, 1968)
Donoghue, Denis: *Words Alone: The Poet T.S. Eliot* (Yale University
    Press, 2000)
Scott, Robert Ian: 'The Waste Land Eliot Didn't Write', *Times
    Literary Supplement*, 8 December 1995
Spender, Stephen: *Eliot* (Fontana, 1975)

Freud, Sigmund: *The Ego and the Id* (Norton, 1990)
Gay, Peter: *Freud: A Life for our Time* (Little, 2006)
Groddeck, Georg: *The Book of the It* (introduction by Lawrence
    Durrell, Vision Press, 1949)

Fitzgerald, F. Scott: *The Great Gatsby* (introduction by Matthew J.
    Bruccoli, Scribners, 1991)
Long, Robert Emmet: *The Achieving of* The Great Gatsby (Bucknell
    University Press, 1979)

Milne, A.A.: *Winnie-the-Pooh* (Methuen, 1926)
Thwaite, Ann: *A.A. Milne, His Life* (Faber, 1990)

Hemingway, Ernest: *The Sun Also Rises* (Granada, 1976)

Berg, A. Scott: *Max Perkins, Editor of Genius* (Hamish Hamilton, 1979)

Bruccoli, Matthew J: *Scott and Ernest* (Random House, 1978)

Corral, Carmen: 'The Textual History of The Sun Also Rises' (Sigma Tau Delta Convention, St Louis 1999, http://www.bama.ua.edu/~sigmatau/texts/sun.html)

Meyers, Jeffrey: *Hemingway* (Macmillan, 1985)

Lawrence, D.H.: *The Escaped Cock* (Black Sparrow, 1975)

Sagar, Keith: *D.H. Lawrence: Life into Art* (Viking, 1985)

Sagar, Keith: *The Art of D.H. Lawrence* (Cambridge University Press, 1966)

West, Nathanael: *Miss Lonelyhearts* (Penguin, 1966)

Martin, Jay: *Nathanael West* (Secker and Warburg, 1971)

Cain, James M.: *The Postman Always Rings Twice* (Penguin, 1954)

Cain, James M: *Three of a Kind* (introduction by James M. Cain, Knopf, 1944)

Madden, David: *James M. Cain* (Twayne, 1970)

Cummings, E.E.: *No Thanks* (introduction by Richard S Kennedy, Liveright, 1978)

Friedman, Norman: 'Not "e.e. cummings" Revisited', *Spring* 5 (1996).

Sawyer-Lauçanno, Christopher: *E.E. Cummings: A Biography* (Methuen, 2005)

Orwell, George: *Nineteen Eighty-Four* (introduction by Ben Pimlott, Penguin, 2000)

Crick, Bernard: *George Orwell, A Life* (Penguin, 1980)

Rodden, John: *George Orwell: The Politics of Literary Reputation* (Transaction, 2002)

Taylor, D.J.: *Orwell, The Life* (Chatto & Windus, 2003)

Lewis, C.S.: *The Lion, the Witch and the Wardrobe* (Collins, 1997)

Green, Roger Lancelyn and Hooper, Walter: *C.S. Lewis, A Biography* (Collins, 1974)

Lewis, C.S.: *Letters to Children* (Collins, 1985)

Lewis, C.S.: *Of Other Worlds* (Harcourt Brace Jovanovich, 1966)
Wilson, A.N.: *C.S. Lewis, A Biography* (Collins, 1990)

Beckett, Samuel: *Waiting for Godot* (Faber, 1979)
Bair, Deirdre: *Samuel Beckett: A Biography* (Simon & Schuster, 1978)
Esslin, Martin: *The Theatre of the Absurd* (Methuen, 2001)

Nabokov, Vladimir: *Lolita* (Weidenfeld & Nicolson, 1959)
Karlinsky, Simon, ed.: *The Nabokov-Wilson Letters:
  Correspondence between Vladimir Nabokov and Edmund
  Wilson 1940–1971* (Harper and Row, 1979)
Maar, Michael: *The Two Lolitas* (Verso, 2005)

Heller, Joseph: *Catch-22* (Corgi, 1971)
Greenfeld, Josh: ''22 was Funnier than 14', *New York Times Review
  of Books*, March 3, 1968
Nagel, James, ed.: *Critical Essays on* Catch-22 (Dickenson, 1972)
Sorkin, Adam J., ed.: *Conversations with Joseph Heller* (University
  Press of Mississippi, 1993)
J.P. Stern, 'War and the Comic Muse: The Good Soldier Schweik
  and Catch-22', *Comparative Literature*, 20 (1968)

Albee, Edward: *Who's Afraid of Virginia Woolf?* (Penguin, 1971)
Ardolino, Frank: 'Nugent and Thurber's *The Male Animal* and
  Albee's *Who's Afraid of Virginia Woolf?, The Explicator* (Spring
  2003)
Bigsby, Christopher: *Albee* (Oliver & Boyd, 1969)
Gussow, Mel: *Edward Albee: A Singular Journey* (Oberon Books,
  1999)
Woolf, Virginia: 'Lappin and Lapinova', *A Haunted House and
  Other Stories* (Harvest, 2002)

Burgess, Anthony: *A Clockwork Orange* (introduction by Anthony
  Burgess, Norton, 1987)
Biswell, Andrew: *The Real Life of Anthony Burgess* (Picador, 2005)
Burgess, Anthony: 'Clockwork Marmalade', in *A Second Listener
  Anthology*, ed. Karl Miller (British Broadcasting Corporation,
  1973)
Burgess, Anthony: *A Clockwork Orange: A Play With Music*
  (introduction by Anthony Burgess, Hutchinson, 1987)

Pinter, Harold: *The Homecoming* (Methuen, 1966)
Billington, Michael: *The Life and Work of Harold Pinter* (Faber, 1996)
Lahr, John, ed.: *A Casebook on Harold Pinter's 'The Homecoming'* (Davis-Poynter, 1974)

Solanas, Valerie: *S.C.U.M. (Society for Cutting Up Men) MANIFESTO* (introduction by Maurice Girodias, Olympia Press, 1968)
Solanas, Valerie: *SCUM Manifesto* (postscript by Freddie Baer, AK Press, 1997)
Solanas, Valerie: *SCUM Manifesto* (introduction by Avital Ronell, Verso, 2004)
Greer, Germaine: *The Female Eunuch* (Paladin, 1971)

Mishima, Yukio: *The Decay of the Angel* (Vintage, 1990)
Ross, Christopher: *Mishima's Sword* (Harper, 2006)
Stokes, Henry Scott: *The Life and Death of Yukio Mishima* (Penguin, 1975)

Mamet, David: *Oleanna* (Methuen, 1992)
http://www.phmc.state.pa.us/ppet/olebull/page1.asp?
Bigsby, Christopher: *The Cambridge Companion to David Mamet* (Cambridge University Press, 2004)

INDEX

Gary Dexter is a frequent contributor to the books pages of the *Guardian*, the *Sunday Telegraph* and the *Spectator*, and has written columns for *The Times* and the *Erotic Review*. He is also the editor of *Chambers Concise Biographical Dictionary*.